THE

LIFE OF JESUS,

ACCORDING TO HIS ORIGINAL BIOGRAPHERS.

WITH NOTES.

BY

EDMUND KIRKE,

AUTHOR OF "AMONG THE PINES," "PATRIOT BOYS AND PRISON PICTURES," ETC.

BOSTON:
LEE & SHEPARD, PUBLISHERS.
MDCCCLXVII.

J. E. FARWELL & CO.
Stereotypers and Printers,
Congress Street.

TO

THE REVEREND GEORGE T. FLANDERS.

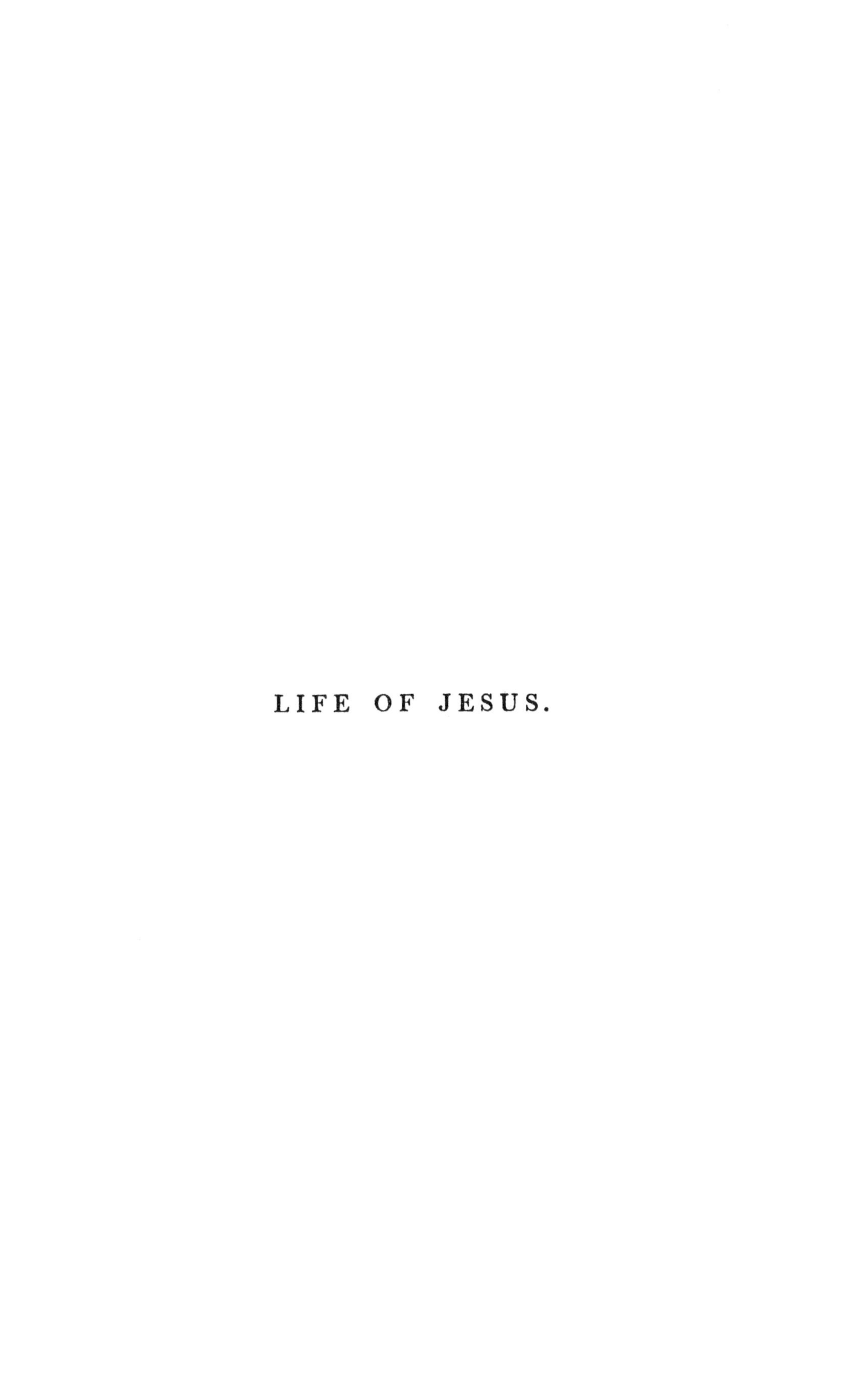

LIFE OF JESUS.

PREFACE.

THIS little volume has grown up in the following manner. Some years since, to acquire a more connected view of the life of Christ than can be gained by a separate reading of the four Evangelists, the writer made, for his private perusal, a monotessaron of the four Gospels, — arranging them so as to relate the same event only once, but to include all the teachings, and all the historical circumstances in one narrative.

Subsequent investigation showed him that he had made some omissions, and many errors in the true order of events; but still, this imperfect compilation, rudely put together in an ordinary Scrap-book, was his only Gospel reading for many years, and from it he obtained so vivid an idea of the daily life of Him who not only "spoke as never man spoke," but who lived as never man lived, that he could almost see him walking the roads, and sitting by the lake-shore of Galilee — and until one does this, he cannot know the wonderful beauty of his most wonderful life.

Not long ago this rude compilation was accidentally seen by a clergyman, whom the writer has the honor to count among his friends, and he recommended that — the text being stripped of the antiquated phraseology of the authorized version, and such brief notes being added as are needed to explain its local and historical allusions — it should be given to the public. This, after much hesitation,—for he is not a teacher, but a learner,—the writer has concluded to do in this volume.

The order of events which has been followed in the text is, in the main, that adopted by Dr. Robinson in his most excellent "Harmony of the four Gospels." The notes are mostly the result of a very wide, but very desultory reading of Biblical authorities; and the source whence particular parts have been drawn, cannot now, in all cases, be readily ascertained. The most that they contain, however, will be found in the Commentaries of Clarke, Whitby, Olshausen, Norton, Tholuck, Campbell, and Rosenmüller; in Horne's Introduction, Jahn's Archæology, Critici Sacra, Calmet's and Smith's Bible Dictionaries, Dr. Thomson's "Land and the Book," Lynch's "Expedition to the Dead Sea," Stanley's "Sinai and Palestine," Neander's "Life of Christ," and Prime's "Tent Life in the Holy Land;" all which works should be read by everyone who would acquire a full knowledge of this most interesting and most important subject.

In the notes no "practical observations," or doctrinal teachings are included. The one who rightly reads the simple record of the life and sayings of Jesus needs no exhortation to a right practice; and, both by his inclination, and by his habits of thought, the writer is unfitted for the exposition — and perhaps also for the understanding — of any system of theology. The grandest truths were uttered by Jesus in the simplest words,— words which the way-faring man, though a fool, can understand,— and he himself said that if any one will do His will, he shall know of the doctrine, whether it be of God, or whether he spoke from himself.

INTRODUCTION.

IN the beginning was the Word, and the Word was with God, and the Word was God. He was in the beginning with God. All things were made by him, and without him nothing was made that was made. In him was life; and the life was the light of men. And the light shone in the darkness; and the darkness received it not.

There was a man sent from God, whose name was John. The same came for a witness, to bear testimony of the Light, that all through him might believe. He was not the Light, but was sent to bear testimony of the Light. The true Light, which shines on every man, came into the world. He was in the world, and the world was made by him, and the world knew him not. He came to his own, and his own received him not. But as many as received him, to them gave he the right to become children of God, even to those that believe on his name: Who are born, not of superior blood, nor by natural generation, nor by the will of man, but of God. And the Word became flesh, and dwelt among us, (and we beheld his glory,—glory as of the only begotten from the Father,) full of grace and truth.

John bore testimony of him, and cried, saying, "This is he of whom I said, He that comes after me, takes rank before me; because he was before me." And out of his fulness have all we received, and grace upon grace. For the law was given by Moses, but grace and truth came by Jesus Christ.

No man has seen God at any time; the only begotten Son, who is in the bosom of the Father, he has made him known.

*John i. 1-18.

PART FIRST.

THE BIRTH AND CHILDHOOD OF JESUS.

TIME — ABOUT THIRTEEN AND A HALF YEARS.

LIFE OF JESUS.

PART FIRST.

IN the reign of Herod, King of Judea, there was a certain priest named Zechariah, of the family of Abijah;* and his wife was of the daughters of Aaron, and her name was Elizabeth. They were both righteous in the sight of God, walking blamelessly in all the commandments and ordinances of the Jewish law. And they had no child, because Elizabeth was barren, and both were well stricken in years. But as Zechariah executed the priest's office, in the order of his course, it fell to him, by lot, to offer incense in the temple at Jerusalem, according to the custom of the priesthood; and a multitude of people were praying in the courts without, at the time of incense. And, as Zechariah entered the holy place, an angel of the Lord appeared to him, standing on the right of the altar of incense, and Zechariah was troubled at the sight, and fear fell upon him. But the angel said, "Fear not, Zechariah, for thy prayer is heard. Thy wife, Elizabeth,

* 1 Chronicles xxiv. 10.

shall bear thee a son; and thou shalt call his name John. He shall give thee joy and gladness, and many will rejoice because of his birth. He will be great in the sight of the Lord, and shall drink neither wine nor strong drink, but be filled with the holy spirit from his mother's womb; and many of the children of Israel will he turn to the Lord their God. He shall go before him in the spirit and power of Elijah, turning the hearts of the fathers to the children, and the disobedient to the wisdom of the just, making ready a people fit for the Lord."*

In the order of his course. — The priesthood was divided by David into twenty-four courses. The several courses began on the Sabbath, and each served for one week. The course of Abijah was the eighth in order, and its service began in the fourth month of the Jewish year, answering to our July. John, therefore, would seem to have been born about the month of May, and Jesus some six months later; probably in September or October.

It fell to him by lot to offer incense. — The various duties of the priests were divided among them by lot. By the first lot was designated who should cleanse the outside of the altar; by the second, who should sacrifice the lamb, sprinkle the blood, and burn and scatter the incense; and by the third, who should ascend the high altar, and lay upon it the members of the victim. Only the High Priest, who belonged to no particular order, was allowed to enter the Holy of Holies, and Zechariah, therefore, must have been in the Holy Place, or the Sanctuary, in which incense was burned, and the people in the court without, probably in "the court of the women."

Nor strong drink. — The common wine of Palestine is not intoxicating, and is drunk freely by all classes of people. The strong drink here referred to, was probably a distillation of

* Malachi iv. 5, 6.

And Zechariah said to the angel, "How shall I know this? I am an old man, and my wife is well stricken in years." The angel answered, "I am Gabriel, who stand in the presence of God, and I am sent to declare to thee these glad tidings; and because thou hast not trusted my words, which will be fulfilled in their season, thou shalt be silent, and not able to speak, till these things are accomplished."

And the people without waited for Zechariah, and wondered that he tarried so long in the temple. And when he came out he could not speak; but they knew that he had seen a vision; for he made signs to them, though he remained speechless. And when the time of his ministration at the temple was ended, he returned to his own house, in the hill-country of Judea.

After this his wife Elizabeth conceived, and kept her condition secret for five months, saying, "Thus the Lord has dealt with me, taking away my reproach among men, at the time of his appointment."

corn, apples, honey, or dates, all of which drinks were in use among the Jews at this time. The East Indians have a liquor they call *sikkir*, which is made by steeping fresh dates in water till it is sweetened; and this is highly intoxicating. From this comes our name cider, and this is supposed to be the strong drink referred to in the text. All fermented liquors were prohibited to the Nazarites and to the Priests during the week they officiated in the temple.

I am Gabriel.—This name denotes, in Hebrew, "The might of the strong God." He was the angel who, five hundred years before, appeared to Daniel, with tidings of the coming Messiah.

My reproach among men.—The Jewish women regarded it as a peculiar happiness to be the lawful mother of children, See Isa. iv. 1; xliv. 3, 4; Lev. xxvi. 9.

And in Elizabeth's sixth month, the angel Gabriel was sent by God to a town of Galilee, called Nazareth, to a virgin betrothed to a man named Joseph, who was of the house of David; and the virgin's name was Mary. And the angel entering in, said to Mary, "Hail, thou who art highly favored! The Lord is with thee. Most blessed art thou among women!" And Mary was troubled at the sight of the angel and at his words, and cast in her mind what the salutation could mean. But the angel said to her, "Fear not, Mary, for thou hast found favor with God. And, lo! thou shalt conceive and bear a son, and call his name Jesus. He shall be great, and the Son of the Highest; and the Lord God will give to him the throne of his father David; and he shall reign over the house of Jacob forever; and of his kingdom there shall be no end."* Then Mary said to the angel, "How can this be, since I know not a man?" And the angel answered, "The Holy Spirit will come upon thee, and the power of the Highest will overshadow thee, so that the holy thing which shall be born of thee will be the Son of God. And, lo! Elizabeth, thy kinswoman, she also has conceived a son in her old age, and this is the sixth month with her who was called barren. For with God nothing is impossible." And Mary said, "Behold the handmaid of the Lord. Let it be to me as thou hast said," And the angel left her.

Then Mary departed in haste, and went into the hill-country, to a town of Juda, and entering the house

Hill-country — The mountain region near Jerusalem. Rob-

* Micah iv. 7.

of Zechariah, saluted Elizabeth. And when Elizabeth heard her salutation, the babe leaped in her womb; and being filled with the Holy Spirit she cried out, with a loud voice, "Most blessed art thou among women, and blessed is the fruit of thy womb! And whence is this that the mother of my Lord should come to me? For, lo! as the voice of thy salutation sounded in my ears, the babe in my womb leaped for joy. And blessed is she who believes that what has been told her by the Lord will be accomplished."

Then Mary said,*

"My soul magnifies the Lord,

And my spirit rejoices in God my Saviour.

For he has regarded the low estate of his handmaiden: and lo! from henceforth all generations shall call me blessed.

For he that is mighty has done to me great things; and holy is his name.

And His mercy is on them that fear him, from generation to generation.

He has made strong his arm; he has scattered the proud in the imagination of their hearts.

He has cast down the mighty from their thrones, and exalted those of low degree.

He has filled the hungry with good things, and the rich he has sent empty away.

inson supposes *Juda* to be a softened form of Juta, or Juttah, a city of the priests in the neighborhood of Carmel. It is about sixty miles from Nazareth, and still exists under the same name.

* See Psalm xxxlv, 3. 1 Sam. ii. 2—10 2. Sam. vii, 26.

He has helped Israel his servant that his mercy may be remembered.

As he said to our fathers, to Abram, and to his seed, for ever."

And Mary abode with Elizabeth about three months, and then returned to her own home.

When Elizabeth's full time came she brought forth a son; and her neighbors and kindred, having heard of the great mercy that the Lord had shown her, rejoiced with her; and coming on the eighth day to circumcise the child, they called him Zechariah, after the name of his father. But his mother said—

"Not so, he shall be called John."

And they said to her, There is none of thy kindred called by this name."

And they made signs to his father, how he would have him called.

And asking for a writing-table, he wrote, "His name is John." And they all wondered.

And his mouth was opened immediately, and his tongue loosed, and he spoke, praising God.

And fear came on all that dwelt round about: and all this was noised abroad through all the hill-country of Judea.

After the name.—The first born son was commonly called after his father.

A writing table.—Before the invention of paper, a small table, covered with wax, was used for ordinary writing. The pen was an iron stile with which characters were traced in the wax. At the present time, children in Barbary are learned to write on a smooth thin board, smeared over with whiting, which may be rubbed off, or renewed at pleasure.

And all that heard laid these things up in their minds, saying, "What manner of child will this be!" And the favor of the Lord was on him.

And his father Zechariah being filled with the Holy Spirit prophesied, saying,

"Blessed be the Lord the God of Israel; for he has visited and redeemed his people,

And has raised up a horn of salvation for us, in the house of his servant David:

As he promised by the mouth of his holy prophets, who have been since the world began:

That we should be saved from our enemies, and from the hand of all that hate us;

To perform the mercy promised to our fathers, and to remember his holy covenant;

The oath which he swore to our father Abraham,

That he would grant to us, that we, being delivered from our enemies, might serve him without fear,

In holiness and righteousness before him, all the days of our life.

And thou, child, shalt be called the Prophet of the Highest, for thou shalt go before the face of the Lord to prepare his ways.

To give his people knowledge of salvation by the remission of their sins.

Through the tender mercy of our God; whereby the dayspring from on high has visited us,

Horn of salvation. — The horn is the emblem of power; for in that, lies the strength of an animal. It is probable that allusion is here made to the horns of the altar. The altar was a place of refuge and safety, and whoever laid hold on its horns was regarded as under Divine protection.

The day spring from on high, might, perhaps be more literally rendered, "the dawning of the day from heaven."

To give light to them that sit in darkness and in the shadow of death, to guide our feet into the way of peace."

And the child grew, and waxed strong in spirit, and was in the deserts till the time of his showing to Israel.*

The birth of Jesus Christ was on this wise: After his mother Mary was betrothed to Joseph, before they came together, she was found to be with child by the Holy Spirit. Then Joseph to whom she was betrothed being a good man, and not willing to make her a public example, purposed to put her away privately. But while he had this in mind, an angel of the Lord appeared to him in a dream, and said, "Joseph, thou son of David, fear not to take Mary as thy wife: for that which is conceived in her is of the Holy Spirit. And she will bear a son, and thou shalt call his name JESUS: for he will save his people from their sins."

All this was done, to fulfil what had been spoken of the Lord by the prophet, saying, "Lo, a virgin will conceive and bring forth a son, and they will call his name Emmanuel, which being interpreted is, God with us." Then Joseph awaking from sleep, did as the angel of the Lord had bidden, and took home his wife:

By, *was in the deserts*, nothing more is probably meant than that John lived a secluded life among his kindred, in the mountain region near Jerusalem, until the beginning of his public ministry.

A public example. — The punishment to which Mary was liable was death by stoning. See Lev. xx. 10; Eze. xvi. 38. 40; John viii. 5.

* Luke i. 1-80.

and knew her not till she had brought forth her first-born son: and he called his name JESUS.*

Now in those days there went forth a decree from Cesar Augustus, that a census should be taken of all the world. (And this census, was first made when Cyrenius was governor of Syria.) And all went to be enrolled, every one to his own town. And Joseph also went up from Galilee, from the town of Nazareth, to Judea, to the city of David, called Bethlehem, — because he was of the house and lineage of David, — to be enrolled with Mary, his betrothed wife, she being great with child. And while they were there, her full time came to be delivered; and she brought forth her first-born son, and wrapping him in swathing-bands, laid him in a stable; because there was no room for them in the inn.

A decree from Cesar Augustus. — In the year B. C. 63., Pompey made Judea tributary to the Roman Empire, and though Herod was styled King, he was altogether dependent on the Emperor.

Bethlehem — Is one of the oldest towns of Palestine, and has still a population of about 3000. The town is about six miles south of Jerusalem, and is built on a long ridge of pure limestone, with a deep valley at the North, and another at the South. Its houses have a substantial appearance, and over the cave where tradition locates the birth of Jesus, is a church and convent, in whose vaults lamps are kept continually burning. Here Jerome is said to have lived thirty years, and to have made the Vulgate translation of the Bible. The adjacent country is of great fertility, and celebrated for the variety and richness of its productions.

In a stable. — The word in the original means the place

* Matt. I. 18-25.

And in the same country certain shepherds were watching their flocks in the fields by night. And lo, an angel of the Lord appeared to them, and a bright light shone round them; and they were greatly afraid. But the angel said to them, "Fear not: for behold, I bring you tidings of great joy, which shall be to all people; for to-day a Saviour is born, in the city of David, who is Christ the Lord. And this will be a sign to you; you shall find the babe wrapped in swathing-bands, lying in a stable." And suddenly there was with the angel a multitude of the heavenly host praising God, and saying, "Glory to God in the highest, and on earth peace, good will toward men."

And when the angels had gone away from them to heaven, the shepherds said one to another, "Let us go now to Bethlehem, and see this that has come to pass, which the Lord has made known to us." And they went with haste, and found Mary and Joseph, and the babe lying in the stable. And when they had

where cattle or camels were lodged. Justin Martyr, in the second century, spoke of Christ's birth as having taken place "in a certain cave very close to the village;" and though there is nothing to sustain the supposition that the cave now covered by the Church of the Nativity is the true locality, there is no improbability in the idea that this stable was in a cave, for at the present day, caves in the East are sometimes used as stables.

In the fields by night. — It was customary with the Jews to send their flocks into the mountains during the summer, and to take them up when the cold weather began, — late in October or early in November. They were guarded by shepherds, and the fact that these men were then "abiding in the fields," shows that the birth of Jesus was prior to the month of December.

seen it, they made known abroad what had been told them concerning the child. And all who heard wondered at what was told them by the shepherds. But Mary kept all these things, and pondered them in her heart. And the shepherds returned, glorifying and praising God for all they had heard and seen, as had been told them.

And when eight days had come for the circumcising of the child, he was called JESUS, the name given him by the angel, before he was conceived in the womb. And when the time for their purification according to the law of Moses, had come, they brought him to Jerusalem, to present him to the Lord: (as it is written in the law of the Lord, Every male that openeth the womb shall be called holy to the Lord;) and to offer a sacrifice according to that which is said in the law of the Lord, a pair of turtle-doves, or two young pigeons.

And lo! there was a man in Jerusalem, whose name was Simeon; he was just and devout, waiting for the consolation of Israel: and the Holy Spirit was upon him. And it had been revealed to him by the Holy Spirit, that he should not see death, before he had seen the Lord's Christ. And led by the Spirit he came into the temple; and when the parents of the child Jesus brought him in to do for him after the custom of

Their purification. — For forty days after the birth of a male child, the Jewish mother was considered impure, and not allowed to enter the temple, or to engage in public religious exercises.

A pair of turtle-doves. — This was the offering of the poor; from those who were able, a lamb was required for a burnt-offering, and a dove for a sin-offering.

the law, he took him in his arms, and blessed God, saying, "Lord, now lettest thou thy servant depart in peace, according to thy word: for mine eyes have seen thy salvation, which thou hast prepared to set before all nations, — a light to enlighten the Gentiles, and to be the glory of thy people Israel." And Joseph and his mother were filled with wonder at these things being spoken of him.

And Simeon blessed them, and said to Mary his mother, "Behold, this child is set for the fall and rising again of many in Israel; and for a sign which shall be spoken against; (yea, a sword shall pierce thine own soul also;) that the thoughts of many hearts may be revealed."

And there was one Anna, a prophetess, the daughter of Phanuel, of the tribe of Asher: of a great age, who had lived with a husband seven years from her virginity. And she was a widow of about fourscore and four years; who never left the temple, but served God with fastings and prayers night and day. She also coming in that instant, gave thanks to the Lord, and spoke of him to all that looked for redemption in Jerusalem.*

And after this Joseph and Mary returned with the child to Bethlehem, and lo! wise men from the east came to Jerusalem, saying, "Where is he that is born king

Wise men from the East. — The Septuagent translation of the Scriptures, which was made at Alexandria, B. C., about 280, had spread among the eastern nations a general expectation that a remarkable personage was to appear about this time, in Judea. This expectation is spoken of, by Suetonius

* Luke ii. 1-38.

of the Jews? for we have seen his star in the east, and have come to worship him." When Herod the king heard of this, he was greatly moved, and all Jerusalem with him. And gathering all the chief priests and doctors of the law together, he inquired of them where Christ was to be born. And they answered him, "In Bethlehem of Judea: for thus it is written by the prophet. 'And thou Bethlehem, in the land of Judah art not the least among the princes of Judah, for out of thee shall come a Governor, who shall rule my people Israel.'"

Then Herod having privately called the wise men, inquired of them what time the star appeared, and

and Tacitus, Roman historians, and also by the Jews, Philo and Josephus. These wise men were Eastern priests, devoted to the study of religion, philosophy, and astronomy; and it is natural to suppose that they were acquainted with the Jewish prediction. It is not necessary to believe that the celestial appearance which they saw, was a star; for it is said that "it went before them, and stood over where the young child was." It was probably a "great light," such as that which shone about the shepherds, and is called in the common version the "glory of the Lord."

Then Herod. — This Herod was of Idumean descent, and the second son of Antipater — made procurator of Judea, B. C., 47. When but fifteen years old he received the government of Galilee, and when Antony came to Syria, six years later, was, with his older brother, appointed tetrarch of Judea. Forced to abandon Judea the next year by the invasion of the Parthians, he fled to Rome, where he was well received by Antony and Octavian, and was made by the Roman Senate, King of the Jews. In the year B. C., 37, with the aid of the Romans, he took Jerusalem, and established his authority throughout his dominions. His reign was not disturbed by external troubles; but his domestic life, and internal admin-

4

sent them to Bethlehem, saying, "Go, search diligently for the young child, and when you have found him, bring me word, that I also may come and do him homage." Having heard the King, they departed, and, lo, the star which they had seen in the east, went before them till it stood over where the young child was. When they saw the star, they rejoiced with great joy; and coming into the house, found the young child with Mary his mother, and falling down before him they paid him homage; and opening their treasures, presented him gifts,—gold, and frankincense, and myrrh. And being divinely warned in a dream not to return to Herod, they went back totheir own country another way.

And when they had gone, lo! the angel of the Lord appeared to Joseph in a dream, and said, "Arise, take the young child and his mother, and flee to Egypt, and remain there until I bring thee word: for

istration, were stained with the foulest crimes. He put to death, with many others, his wife, Mariamne, her grandfather, her mother, and two of his own sons, one of whom he caused to be executed only five days before he died. He practised unheard-of barbarities on his subjects, and the monstrous acts of cruelty which are recorded of him show that he was fully capable of the slaughter of the children at Bethlehem. While on his death-bed, he ordered all the nobles of Judea to be assembled at Jericho, and confining them in the circus, gave direction for their execution, saying that every Jewish family, though unwillingly, should mourn at his death. He died of a most painful and loathsome disease at Jericho, between two and four years, as is supposed, after the birth of Christ. Then the sceptre "departed from Judah," and it was ruled by tetrarchs, without the power, or royal magnificence of Herod.

Herod will seek the young child to destroy him." And he arose, took the young child and his mother, and went by night to Egypt; and was there until the death of Herod: to fulfil what was spoken by the Lord through the prophet, "Out of Egypt have I called my son."

Then Herod, seeing that he was mocked of the wise men, was greatly enraged, and sent and destroyed all the children that were in Bethlehem, and in all its borders, who were two years old and under, according to the time which he had ascertained from the wise men. Thus was fulfilled what was spoken by Jeremiah the prophet, "In Ramah a voice was heard, lamentation, and weeping, and great mourning. Rachel weeping for her children, and would not be comforted because they were not." But after the death of Herod, lo! an angel of the Lord appeared in a dream to Joseph in Egypt, and said, "Arise, and take the child and his mother, and go to the land of Israel; for they are dead who sought the young child's life." And he arose, and took the child and his mother; and came to the land of Israel. But having heard that Archelaus was ruling in Judea in the place of his father Herod, he was afraid to go there: and being divinely warned in a dream, he turned aside and went to Galilee; and dwelt in a town called Nazareth; to fulfil what was spoken by the prophets. "He will be called a Nazarene."* And the child grew, and waxed strong in spirit, being full of wisdom; and the grace of God was upon him.

Now his parents went to Jerusalem every year at the

* Matt 2. 1—23.

feast of the passover. And when Jesus was twelve years old, they went up according to the custom of the feast, and remained till it was over. And as they returned, the child Jesus stayed behind in Jerusalem. And Joseph and his mother knew it not; but supposing that he was in the company, they went on, a day's journey, and sought him among their relatives and acquaintance. But not finding him, they turned back to Jerusalem, seeking him. And on the third day they found him in the temple, sitting in the midst of the doctors, both hearing them, and asking them questions. And all who

Feast of the Passover. — This was the first of the three great annual feasts of the Jews. It continued eight days, and took place at the full of the moon which occurred at the vernal equinox. It was instituted to commemorate the passing over of the houses of the Israelites, when the first-born of the Egyptians were destroyed: and at it the first-fruits of the barley harvest were offered. The Pentecost, occurred seven weeks, or fifty days later, and commemorated the giving of the Law. At this feast, the first-fruits of the wheat harvest were offered. The Tabernacles, occurred near the end of September, or beginning of October, when the produce of the fields and vineyards had been gathered. It commemorated the sojourn of the Israelites, in tents or tabernacles, in the desert, and was observed as a thanksgiving for the blessings of the year. Every adult Jew, dwelling in Judea, was obliged to attend at each of these feasts, and the numbers at such times assembled at Jerusalem, often exceeded two millions. The people on their way to and from the festivals, travelled in caravans, whole families often going together, and it was no doubt, among one of these caravans, that Mary and her husband sought the boy Jesus, sorrowing.

The Doctors, — elsewhere called Scribes, were the authorized expounders of the sacred books of the Jews. Though the Law made it the duty of parents to teach their children its

heard him were astonished at his understanding and his answers. And when his parents saw him, they were amazed; and his mother said: "Son, why hast thou thus dealt with us? thy father and I have sought thee sorrowing." And he said to them, "How is it that you have sought me? know you not that I must be about my father's business?" But they understood not what he said to them. And he went down

precepts and principles, the education of the common people consisted of little more than the learning of texts written on phylacteries, the committing to memory of endless genealogies, and such scanty teaching as was given in the synagogues. Of the Scribes, however, a certain sort of erudition was required. At five years of age the child destined for this office was learned to read, at ten, he began the study of the Mishna, and at thirteen was expected to enter the school of some Rabbi at Jerusalem. If poor, he was supported at this school by the synagogue of his town or village. The education was chiefly catechetical, the pupil asking questions and the teacher examining the scholar; and the class-room was a chamber in the Temple, or the Private school of the Rabbi. In teaching, the Rabbi occupied a high chair, and the pupils sat about him, on lower benches, — the younger on the ground, and literally "at his feet." Physical science formed a part of the course of instruction; but much more attention was given to the Scriptures, and to the written "traditions of the elders." At the age of thirty, the pupil was solemnly inducted into the "chair of the Scribes," by the imposition of hands, and then was given tablets on which to note down the sayings, of the wise, and, the "key of knowledge," (Luke xi. 52.) with which he was to open and shut the treasures of Divine wisdom. The Scribe might rise to the high places, become an arbitrator of family disputes (Luke xii. 14), the head of a school, a member of the Sanhedrim; or he might sink into an humble transcriber of the Scriptures, or into a

with them to Nazareth, and was subject to their direction; but his mother kept all these things in her

still humbler notary, writing out contracts of sale, or espousals, and bills of repudiation. The more distinguished of the order occupied the highest social position, and in the time of Christ, their passion for distinction was insatiable. Combining within themselves nearly all the energy and thought of Judaism, the close hereditary caste of the priesthood was powerless to compete with them; and, unless a priest became also a Scribe, he remained in obscurity. Under these influences the character of the order was marked by a deep and incurable hypocrisy, which merited the scathing invectives of Jesus. See Smith. Bible Dictionary, and Adam Clark, *in loco.*

In the midst of the Doctors. — When teaching in public the Scribes sat on benches of a semi-circular form, raised above their auditors and disciples, so that Jesus was no doubt literally seated "in their midst."

Nazareth — "was a little town, situated in a fold of land broadly open at the summit of the group of mountains which closes on the north the plain of Esdraelon. The population is now from three to four thousand, and it cannot have varied very much. It is quite cold in winter, and the climate is very healthy. Like all the Jewish villages of the time, the town was a mass of dwellings built without pretension to style, and must have presented that poor and uninteresting appearance which is offered by villages in Semitic countries. The houses from all that appears, did not differ much from those cubes of stone, without exterior or interior elegance, which now cover the richest portion of the Lebanon, and which in the midst of vines and fig-trees, are nevertheless very pleasant. The envirous, moreover, are charming, and no place in the world was so well adapted to dreams of absolute happiness. Antoninus Martyr, at the end of the sixth century, draws an enchanting picture of the fertility of the environs, which he compares to paradise. Some valleys on the western side fully justify his description. The fountain about which the life and gayety of the little town formerly centered, has been destroyed; its broken channels now give but a turbid water.

heart. And Jesus increased in wisdom and stature, and in favor with God and man.

With the exception of something sordid and repulsive which Ismalism carries with it everywhere, it did not, in the time of Jesus, differ much from what it is to-day. We see the streets in which he played when a child, in the stony paths, or the little squares which separate the dwellings. The house of Joseph, without doubt, closely resembled those poor shops, lighted by the door, serving at once for the work-bench, as kitchen and as bedroom, having for furniture a mat, some cushions on the ground, one or two earthern vessels and a painted chest.

The horizon of the town is limited, but if we ascend a little to the plateau swept by a perpetual breeze, which commands the highest houses, the prospect is splendid. To the west are unfolded the beautiful lines of Carmel, terminating in an abrupt point which seems to plunge into the sea. Then stretch away the double summit which looks down upon Megiddo, the mountains of Gilboa, the picturesque little group with which are associated the graceful and terrible memories of Solam and of Endor, and Thabor with its finely-rounded form, which antiquity compared to a breast. Through a depression between the mountains of Solam and Thabor, are seen the valley of the Jordan and the high plains of Perœa which form a continuous line in the east. To the north, the mountains of Safed, sloping towards the sea, hide St Jean d' Acre, but disclose the gulph of Khaifa. Such was the horizon of Jesus. This enchanted circle, the cradle of the kingdom of God, represented the world to him for years. His life, even, went little beyond the limits familiar to his childhood; for, beyond, to the north, you almost see upon the slope of Hermon, Cesarea Philippi, his most advanced point into the Gentile world; and to the south, you feel behind these already less cheerful mountains of Samaria, sad Judea, withered as by a burning blast of destruction and of death." — RENAN.

Subject to their direction. — The early years of Jesus are

* Luke 2. 40-52.

veiled in obscurity. It is known that his parents were poor, (Luke ii. 24) that his reputed father was an artisan, that he, himself, wrought at his father's trade, (Mark vi. 3.) and that he was not trained in any of the schools of the Jewish nation; (John vii. 15., Matt xiii. 54,) but beyond this, all is conjecture. He probably understood no other language than the Syro-Chaldaic and the ancient Hebrew; and had no other learning than the Old Testament, and the Pharisaic traditions. To attempt to trace the secret of his power to the influence of his time, or the culture of the schools of his nation, as has been done, is worse than useless, for he rises above all times and all schools, and in his world-creative and world-transforming power stands alone in history. Like the New Jerusalem which he founded, "he descended from God out of heaven.

PART SECOND.

INTRODUCTION TO CHRIST'S PUBLIC MINISTRY.

TIME — ABOUT ONE YEAR.

LIFE OF JESUS.

PART SECOND.

IN the fifteenth year of the reign of Tiberius Cesar, Pontius Pilate being governor of Judea, and Herod Antipas tetrarch of Galilee, and his brother Philip tetrarch of Iturea and the country of Trachonitis, and Lysanias the tetrarch of Abilene, while Annas and Caiaphas were high priests, the word of God came to John, the son of Zechariah in the Desert; and he went through all the country about the Jordan, preaching the baptism of repentance for the remission of sins; and saying, "Repent, for the kingdom of heaven

Desert.—This was a rough, mountainous, and sparsely settled region, lying along the western margin of the Dead Sea and the river Jordan. It contained some villages, and also many scattered inhabitants; but a considerable portion of it would properly be called a wilderness. (1 Sam. xxv. 1. 2.) Josephus relates that about this time many devout men among the Jews, disgusted with the wickedness of the age, retired to desert places, and there, becoming teachers of a purer morality, gathered disciples about them: he, however, mentions none by name but the Baptist.

The phrase, kingdom of heaven,—might be as literally rendered, "The reign of God."

is at hand:" This was in fulfilment of what had been written by Isaiah the prophet, "The voice of one crying in the wilderness, Prepare ye the way of the Lord, make his paths straight. Every valley must be filled, and every mountain and hill be levelled down; the crooked ways be made straight, and the rough places smooth; that all men may see the salvation from God."

And John wore raiment of camel's hair, and had a leathern girdle about his loins; and his food was locusts and wild honey. And vast multitudes from

Prepare ye the way of the Lord. — It was the custom of Eastern monarchs, when setting out on an expedition, or undertaking a journey through a desert country, to send messengers before them, to open the passes, level the ways, and prepare all things for their passage. The roads in Palestine are wretched at their best estate; but the custom of the farmers to gather up the stones from the fields and cast them into the highways, renders them dangerous, and, at times, almost impassable. Dr. Thomson relates that when Ibrahim Pasha some years ago, proposed to visit the Lebanon, the emeers and sheikhs sent forth a general proclamation, somewhat in the style of this passage, directing all the inhabitants to assemble along the proposed route, and prepare the way before him. The same was done in 1845, on a grander scale, when the Sultan visited Brusa. The stones were gathered out of the roads, "the crooked ways were made straight, and the rough places smooth."

Camel's hair. — A coarse, cheap cloth is still made in the East, from the long, shaggy hair of the camel, and is extensively worn by the poorer classes. It was the common dress of the Jewish prophets.

Locusts and wild honey. — Burckhardt says, "All the Bedawins of Arabia are accustomed to eat locusts. At Medina and Tayf are locust shops where these animals are sold by meas-

Jerusalem, and Judea, and from all the region round about, went out to him and were baptized in the Jordan, confessing their sins.

But when he saw that many of the Pharisees and Sadducees had come to his baptism, he said to

ure. In Egypt and Nubia they are eaten by only the poorest beggars." "The Arabs in preparing them as food, throw them alive into boiling water with which a good deal of salt is mixed. After a few minutes they are taken out, and dried in the sun; the head, feet and wings are torn off, and the bodies are cleansed from salt, and perfectly dried." Locusts are not now eaten in Syria, except by the lowest of the Bedawins, and are generally regarded with disgust and loathing. When eaten, they are sometimes fried in butter, and mixed with wild honey, and this honey is still plentifully gathered from the trees and rocks of the desert in which the Baptist sojourned.

Baptized. — Baptism was in use among the Jews before the time of John, as the rite of initiation to Gentile proselytes. It was regarded as a typical washing away of the defilements of heathenism.

Pharisees and Sadducees. — The Pharisees were the most numerous and influential sect among the Jews. They are supposed to have originated about three centuries before Christ, when the national institutions of Judea were threatened with destruction from the influx of Greek manners and opinions; and their object was to keep the Jews a separate people. Hence their name, which denotes *separated.* Their intense patriotism made them at once popular, and they soon acquired a controlling influence in the nation. They formed a sort of society, whose members were held to a strict observance of certain rules; and they looked with contempt on the middle and lower classes who did not belong to their order. These rules were mainly drawn from the numberless "traditions of the elders," which had accumulated about the law of Moses, and some of them were of the most trivial and ridicu-

them, "O brood of vipers, who has warned you to flee from the wrath to come? Bring forth fruits worthy of repentance; and say not to yourselves, 'We have Abraham for our father,' for I tell you that God is able of these stones to raise up children to Abraham. Now the axe is laid to the root of the trees: and every

lous character; but they were regarded as of vital importance, and their violation was attended with the most severe religious penalties. An egg, laid on a festival day, they held, could not be eaten, and an animal slaughtered by a heathen, was as unfit for food as one which had died of disease. They were proud, formal, and self-righteous; but not generally wealthy or given to luxury. Their besetting sin appears to have been hypocrisy, and their affectation of extreme sanctity, no doubt, gave them their great influence among the Jewish people, whose religion had educated them in formalism. According to Josephus, they believed in the immortality of the soul, and the resurrection of the body at the last day. They held, too, that the soul of a good man, might pass (transmigrate) into another body; but that the soul of the bad underwent eternal torment; and that some, but not all, things are the work of fate: that angels, good and bad, interfere in human affairs, and that they were justified by their own observance of the law, and by the merits of Abraham, who, by his obedience had secured the peculiar favor of God to his descendants. The *Sadducees*, are supposed to have originated with Zadok, a Jewish doctor, who lived about two hundred and fifty years before Christ, and their leading tenet seems to have been the denial of all that the Pharisees affirmed; they, however, accepted the five books of Moses. They were few in number; but powerful from their wealth and social position.

The axe is laid to the root of the trees. — The fellaheen of Palestine at the present day, in felling trees, clears away the earth, and lays the axe at the very roots; and he values only such trees as bear fruit. All others he cuts down as cumberers of the ground.

tree which brings not forth good fruit will be cut down, and cast into the fire." And they said to him, "What then must we do?" He answered, "Let him that has two tunics, give to him that has none; and let him that has food, do likewise. Even tax-gatherers came to him to be baptized, and they said, "Master,

Tax-gatherers. — As early as the second Punic War, the Roman senate found it convenient to farm the direct taxes and customs of the empire to capitalists, who undertook to pay a given sum into the treasury, and so received the name of *publicani.* These capitalists generally resided in Rome, and had subordinates living in the provinces, who had under them customs officers employed in the actual collection of the taxes from the people. These latter were generally, natives of the districts in which they lived. The capitalists were an influential class, and demanded severe laws for the enforcement of levies, and put every such law in execution. Their agents were encouraged in the most fraudulent and vexatious exactions, and a remedy was next to impossible. The underlings of these agents also overcharged systematically (Luke iii. 13), brought false charges of smuggling in hopes of obtaining hush-money (Luke xix. 8), and resorted to every possible mode of extortion. All this brought them into universal disfavor, and in Judea and Galilee, there were peculiar circumstances of exaggeration. The Jews bore the Roman yoke with great impatience, and were told by many of the Scribes, that the paying of tribute was unlawful, (Matt. xxii. 17.) The native tax-gatherer was therefore held in great detestation. He was not only an extortioner, but a traitor and apostate, defiled by intercourse with the heathen, and the willing tool of the Roman oppressor, and so was cast out of society, and classed with sinners,—thieves, adulterers, and other abandoned characters. He is said by some, to have been forbidden to enter the temple, or any synagogue, and not to have been allowed to engage in public prayer, to hold judicial office, or to give evidence in courts of Justice. In Persia, at

what must we do?" And he said to them, "Exact no more than is appointed you." And the soldiers also demanded, "What must we do?" He said to them, "Do violence to no one, nor accuse any falsely; and be content with your wages." And while the people were in expectation, and all were questioning whether John were the Christ, or not; he said to them, "I indeed am baptizing with water; but One comes after me who is mightier than I, his sandals I am not worthy to bear: he will baptize you with the Holy Spirit and with fire; for his fan is in his hand, and he will thoroughly cleanse his floor, and

the present day, the same system of farming taxes is practised, and under it the same abuses exist.

Soldiers. — Herod Antipas was at this time at war with Aretas, King of Arabia Petræa, and these may have been Jewish soldiers; but as Judea was garrisoned by the Roman legions, they were more likely Romans. The *wages* of this class were about three cents a day, with a meagre ration, in addition.

His sandals I am not worthy to bear. — Allusion is here made to the custom for servants to remove their master's sandals, on his entering his dwelling. The same custom still exists among the Mohammedans.

His Fan. — Threshing, among the Jews, was done in an open space, without walls or covering, trodden down as hard as a floor, and usually on elevated ground to take advantage of the wind in winnowing. The grain was trodden out, by oxen, or beaten with flails; and was then separated from the chaff by a fan — a fork with several prongs, — which was *held in the hand*, and used to throw up the mingled heap against the wind, when the chaff, being lighter than the wheat was blown away. The chaff, owing to the scarcity of wood, was afterwards gathered, and burned in ovens as fuel.

gather the wheat into his garner; but the chaff he will burn up with unquenchable fire."*

Thus, with many other exhortations, he published the glad-tidings to the people.

Then Jesus came from Galilee to the Jordan to be baptized by John. But John refused him, saying, "I have need to be baptized by you, and come you to me?" But Jesus answered, "Permit it to be so now: for thus must we do to fulfil all righteousness." Then John baptized him. And as Jesus came up out of the water, lo! while he was praying, the heavens were opened, and John saw the Spirit of God descending in a bodily shape, like a dove, and lighting on him: and lo! a voice from heaven said: "This is my beloved Son in whom I am well pleased." And Jesus at this time was about thirty years of age.†

Then Jesus being full of the Holy Spirit, was led into the Desert to be tempted by the devil. And being there forty days and forty nights with the wild beasts, and eating nothing, he afterwards hungered. Then the tempter came to him and said, "If thou art the Son of God, command these stones to become bread." But Jesus answered, it is written, "Man shall not live by bread alone, but by every word that comes from the mouth of God." Then the devil took him to

The heavens were opened. — Stephen speaks of a similar appearance in Acts vii. 56. Livy, in speaking of a supposed like phenomenon, says (Lib. xxii. c. 1.) "the heaven appeared to be rent with a wide chasm, and where it was opened, a great light appeared."

* Matt 3: 1-12. Mark 1: 2-8. Luke 3: 1-18.
† Matt. iii. 13-17. Mark i. 9-11. Luke iii. 20-23.

the holy city, and set him on a pinnacle of the temple, and said to him, "If thou art the Son of God, cast thyself down: for it is written, 'He will give his angels charge over thee, and in their hands they will bear thee up, lest thou dash thy foot against a stone." Jesus said to him, "It is also written, 'Thou shalt not make trial of the Lord thy God.'" Again the devil took him up to a very high mountain, and showing him all the kingdoms of the world, and their glory, in a moment of time; said to him, "All this will I give thee — for it is committed to me, and to whom I will I give it, — if thou wilt fall down and worship me." Then Jesus answered him, "Get thee hence, Satan: for it is written, 'Thou shalt worship the Lord thy God, and him only shalt thou serve.'" Then the devil

The Temptation. — Commentators have vexed themselves to determine the precise part of the temple referred to as the *pinnacle*, and to locate the "exceeding high mountain," from which Jesus was shown "all the kingdoms of the world, and the glory of them;" but all such inquiries would seem to be unnecessary. It cannot be supposed that Jesus was transferred by the Evil One to Jerusalem, and from no mountain in Judea could he have seen a tenth part of the then Roman Empire. The account therefore, cannot be taken literally; but must be understood as a symbolic representation of Christ's mental experience in the Desert. Viewed in this light, it is not only divested of all improbability; but presents internal evidence of being historically true. What more suitable than this silent, solitary preparation for the great work before him — a work no less than the re-creation of a world? and what more natural than his trial by the powers of Evil — powers which every man, even if he deny a personal devil, knows must exert an active and powerful influence in all human affairs.

having ended every temptation, left him for a time, and lo! angels came and ministered to him.*

Now this is the testimony of John. When the Jews sent priests and Levites from Jerusalem, to ask him; "Who are you?" he spoke openly, not refusing to answer, saying, "I am not the Christ." And they asked him; Are you, Elijah?" And he said; "I am not." "Are you that prophet?" And he answered; "No." Then said they to him; "Who then are you? that we may give an answer to those who

The Jews — here referred to, were probably the Sanhedrim, or great council of the nation, a body composed of seventy-two judges, drawn from the chief priests, the scribes, and elders of the people, and presided over by the ruling high priest. The tribunal was instituted about two hundred years before Christ, and till the time when Judea was subjected to the Romans, held the power of life and death. It still had cognizance of all important affairs, and retained the power of trial and sentence in capital cases, but not the right of execution. That was reserved to the Roman governor. John had become widely known. This is evident from the multitudes that flocked to his baptism, and from the presence at Bethany of obscure fishermen from the distant province of Galilee. His wide-spread reputation, is also spoken of by Josephus. Hence, in view of the excitement he was creating, it was natural that the Sanhedrim should desire to know his true character.

I am not the Christ. — Daniel, five hundred years before, had so definitely fixed the date of Christ's advent, that the learned men among the Jews were then in daily expectation of his appearance. It was supposed that Elijah, risen from the dead, would precede him, and, by many, that the prophet spoken of by Moses, in Deut. xviii. 15. would also attend his coming.

* Matt. iv. 1-11. Mark i. 12, 13. Luke iv. 1-13.

sent us. What say you of yourself?" He said; "I am a voice crying in the desert, prepare ye the way of the Lord," as said the prophet Isaiah. And those who were sent, were Pharisees; and they asked him; "Why then, do you baptize? if you are not the Christ, nor Elijah, nor that prophet?" John answered them, "I baptize with water; but there is one among you, whom you know not, he who is coming after me,—whose sandals I am not worthy to unloose."

This took place at Bethany beyond the Jordan, where John was baptizing.

The next day John saw Jesus coming to him, and said, "Behold the Lamb of God, who will take away the sins of the world. This is he, of whom I said; 'After me comes a man who takes rank before me; for he was before me. And I knew him not; but I come baptizing with water that he might be made manifest to Israel."

And John bore this testimony: "I have seen the Spirit descending from heaven like a dove, and resting on him. And I knew him not; but he who sent me to

Why do you baptize?—Baptism was then practised only upon heathen proselytes; John baptized both Jews and Gentiles: hence the question.

Bethany—is the name given to this place in all the oldest MSS. It was located on the Jordan, about twelve miles north of Jericho, and was probably, as the etymology of the word denotes, a small hamlet near a ferry.

I knew him not.—John had lived a secluded life in the desert; therefore, while he cannot be supposed to have been ignorant of the circumstances attending his own, and Christ's birth, it is evident that he would not naturally be personally acquainted with Jesus, who had been pursuing an humble calling in an obscure town of Galilee.

baptize with water, said to me, 'He, on whom thou shalt see the Spirit descending and resting, is he who will baptize with the Holy Spirit. And I have seen, and bear testimony that this is the Son of God."*

The next day, John standing with two of his disciples, saw Jesus as he walked, and said, "Behold! the Lamb of God." And the two disciples hearing what he said, followed Jesus. Then Jesus turning about, and seeing them following, said to them "What seek you?" They answered: "Teacher, where do you dwell?" He said to them, "Come and see." They went and saw where he dwelt; and remained with him that day. It was about the tenth hour. One of the two who heard John and followed Jesus, was Andrew, Simon Peter's brother. He first found his brother Simon, and said to him; "We have found the Messiah;" (that is, the Christ,) and he brought him to Jesus, and he looking on him, said, "You are Simon, the son of Jonah; you shall be called Peter," (which signifies a rock.)

The tenth hour. — The Jews reckoned the day from sunrise, the Romans, as we do, from midnight. The tenth hour, therefore, might have been either ten A. M, or four P. M.

You shall be called Peter. — In Matt. xvi. 18, Jesus explains why he gave this name to Simon, by saying, "upon this rock I will build my church." Peter, though during the life-time of Jesus, weak, hasty, and unstable, showed, after his death, all the strength, firmness, and endurance of a rock. But the application of this name to him shows not only that Jesus possessed that knowledge of men which is the birthright of all royal natures; it also shows that then — at the very beginning of his public career — he had formed the plan, and foreseen the progress of a kingdom which should endure forever.

* John i. 19-32.

The day following, Jesus determined to go into Galilee; and finding Philip, he said to him; "Follow me." Philip was of Bethsaida, the town of Andrew and Peter. Philip met Nathaniel, and said to him; "We have found him of whom Moses in the law, and the prophets wrote, Jesus of Nazareth, the son of Joseph." And Nathaniel said to him; "Can any thing good come out of Nazareth?" Philip answered; "Come and see." Jesus saw Nathaniel coming to him, and said of him; "Behold a true Israelite in whom there is no guile." Nathaniel said to him; "How know you me?" Jesus answered, "Before Philip called you, when you were under the fig-tree, I saw you." Nathaniel answered, "Teacher: you are the Son of

Peter founded the church at Rome, and that church, whatever its corruptions, kept Christianity alive during the dark ages. It is therefore the foundation on which Christ has built; but it is only the foundation. The superstructure is the New Jerusalem he is now erecting, and which is destined to cover the earth, as the waters cover the sea.

Nathaniel — was of Cana in Galilee, a town only nine miles from Nazareth, and that he did not know Jesus, shows that the latter had till now lived a very obscure life.

Can anything good come out of Nazareth? — The Nazarenes, and indeed all the Galileans, were a mixed race, partly of Gentile origin, and were contaminated with many vices. They were proverbially boorish and stupid, and had produced no teachers or prophets. (John vii. 52.) They were held in great contempt by the Jews of Jerusalem.

Fig-tree. — In the warm Eastern countries, this tree grows much larger than in our Southern States, and its broad leaves and thick-spreading branches afford a pleasant shade from the heat of the day. Numerous passages in the rabbinical writers indicate that its shade was a favorite resort for reading, conversation, and prayer.

God, you are the King of Israel." Jesus said to him; "Because I said to you, I saw you under the fig-tree, do you believe? You will see greater things than this. Truly, truly, I say to you; henceforth you will see heaven opened, and the angels of God ascending and descending to the Son of Man."*

And on the third day following, there was a marriage at Cana in Galilee; and the mother of Jesus was there. And Jesus and his disciples were asked to the feast. And the wine having failed, the mother of

King of Israel. — The Jews, understanding the prophecies literally, expected a temporal Messiah, who should free them from the Roman yoke, and give them dominion of the world.

The angels ascending and descending. — This is an evident allusion to the ladder which Jacob saw in his dream. The meaning is, no doubt, that Nathaniel would see such supernatural manifestations as would fully prove that God was with Jesus.

Cana in Galilee — was a small town, about nine miles northeast of Nazareth. It is now called Kânâ, and travellers describe it as situated on an isolated hill, facing to the southeast, and rising boldly from the margin of a wide plain, called Bŭttauf. Deep ravines are on two of its sides, and almost shut it off from the surrounding country. The houses are built of limestone, cut and laid up in a rude fashion, and fragments of water-jars and the ruins of ancient cisterns are scattered about its streets, but the place is deserted, and has not had a human inhabitant within fifty years. It is now the home of the leopard and the wild boar, and its immediate neighborhood is covered with a thick jungle, and is so wild, that it is the favorite hunting-ground of the Bedâwins. Galilee, at this time included all the country south of Phenicia, and north of

* John i. 35-51.

Jesus said to him, "They have no wine." Jesus said to her, "Woman, what have you and I in common? My hour has not yet come." His mother said to the servants, "Whatever he may tell you, do." And six stone water-pots, each holding two or three firkins, were set there to be used for purifications, after the custom of the Jews. Jesus said to the servants, "Fill the pots with water." And they filled them to the brim. Then he said to them, "Draw out now, and bear to the governor of the feast." And they did so.

Samaria, which lay between the Jordan and the Mediterranean.

The wedding feast — among the Jews, often lasted seven or eight days (Gen. xxviii. 27. Judg. xiv. 14). The marriage took place at the house of the bride, the feast which followed, at the house of the bridegroom. The guests were of two kinds, those invited, and those who came without invitation. The latter were expected to bring presents. The governor was a person appointed to provide for the feast, and to superintend the servants, and was required to taste the wine previous to setting it before the guests.

Woman — was a form. of address used in the East, as the word "madam" is with us. It was applied to ladies of rank, even by their servants; and Jesus when on the cross, used it in addressing his mother. In this answer to her, as rendered in the common version, there is an apparent harshness which is not warranted by the context. Her direction to the servants shows that in his apparent denial, she understood a real granting of her request, and it seems also to imply that though this was his first public miracle, she was already acquainted with his extraordinary powers.

Firkins.—The Hebrew *bath*, a measure of about seven and a half gallons, is supposed to be intended. If this be so, the quantity of wine was fully a hundred gallons.

Purifications. — The Jews were *unclean* if they did not wash both before and after eating. This was done in a formal man-

But when the ruler of the feast tasted the water, now become wine, not knowing whence it was, (but the servants who had drawn the water knew,) he called to the bridegroom, saying, "Every one sets on the good wine first: and when men have drunk freely, that which is poorer, but you have kept the good wine till now."

Thus Jesus did his first miracle at Cana in Galilee,

ner, and was, with the washing of cups, pots and brazen vessels, a ritual observance on which the Pharisees laid great stress.

Water now became wine. — The master of the feast detects a difference between this and ordinary wine, and it is not necessary to suppose that the water was actually made into wine; but into a substance closely resembling wine.

A Miracle, — as the etymology of the word denotes, is simply a wonder, or a wonderful work, but, as commonly used, the term is made to mean "an event or effect contrary to the established constitution and course of things." This is doubtless an incorrect definition, and as so defined, the miracle meets a natural incredulity, because Nature observes certain uniform laws, from which, to our eyes, she never appears to deviate: and as she acts uniformly, so far as we see, we have a right to infer that she acts so universally. But might not a miracle be better defined as the action of a higher law, on a lower one, by which the lower is for the time neutralized and suspended? Thus, whenever we lift a hand, we overcome the law of gravity — that is, our will suspends for the time the natural action of matter. We know that Spirit always controls matter. The extent of its control must depend solely on the strength of the will, and may we not suppose that the will of the man who, by a single word, prostrated a band of Roman soldiers, and by a few chance thoughts, scattered here and there among an ignorant people, revolutionized a world, was strong enough to give him unlimited control

and manifested his glory; and his disciples believed in him.

After this he and his mother, and his kinsmen, and disciples, went down to Capernaum; but continued there not many days.*

over dead matter. But similar miracles to Christ's have been done by other men, and this shows that he acted, not in opposition to, but in accordance with real, but as yet hidden, laws of nature. Wherein his miracles differed from those of others, was in their being freer, greater, and done by the natural action of his own will. Peter says, "In the name of Jesus of Nazareth, rise up and walk." Christ says, "Lazarus, come forth." And "Young man, *I* say to thee, arise!"

* John ii. 1-12.

PART THIRD.

THE FIRST PASSOVER, AND SUBSEQUENT EVENTS.

TIME — ONE YEAR.

LIFE OF JESUS.

PART THIRD.

THE passover of the Jews being at hand, Jesus went up to Jerusalem, and he found there those that sold oxen and sheep and doves, and the money-changers sitting in the temple. And making a scourge of small cords, he drove them all out with the sheep and oxen; and poured out the money of the exchangers, overturning their tables; and said to those who sold doves, "Take these things hence; make not my Father's house a house of traf-

Changers of money. — For the convenience of those from a distance, booths were erected in the outer court of the temple, at which everything necessary for the offerings was kept, and where the money-changers had stands to exchange the Roman coin for the Jewish money required for the temple tribute. The leading Pharisees are supposed to have been interested in this traffic. Josephus says that no less than two hundred and forty-six thousand victims were offered at one passover; and as great extortion was practised, large profits must have arisen to the traffickers.

Small cords. — The original implies that this scourge was made of twisted reeds, which, probably, was the ancient material for ropes.

fic." And his disciples called to mind that it had been written, "My zeal for thy house is consuming me."

Then the Jews said to him, "What sign do you show, that you have authority to do this?" Jesus answered, "Destroy this temple, and in three days I will raise it up." Then the Jews said, "Forty and six years has this temple been in building, and will you raise it in three days?" But he spoke of the temple of his body. When, therefore, he had risen from the dead, his disciples remembered that he had said this, and they believed the scripture, and the words which Jesus had spoken.

While Jesus was in Jerusalem at this festival of the passover, many believed in him from seeing his miracles. But he did not trust himself to them, because he knew them all, and needed not that any should tell him, for he knew what is in man.*

And one of the Pharisees named Nicodemus, a ruler of the Jews, came to him by night, and said to him, "Rabbi, we know that you are a teacher come from God; for no man could do these miracles that you do, unless God were with him." Jesus answered him, "Truly, truly, I say to you; unless a man be born

Zeal for thy house. — Psalms lxix. 9.

Forty and six years. — Herod began the rebuilding of the temple sixteen years before the birth of Christ. The work on the main building was completed in nine years and a half, but the outbuildings were unfinished at this date, and were not completed till the time of Agrippa. Jesus at this time was thirty years old.

* John ii. 13-25.

anew, he cannot see the kingdom of God." Nicodemus said to him. "How can a man be born when he is old? can he enter again into his mother's womb, and be born?" Jesus answered, "Truly, truly, I tell you, unless one be born of water, and of the Spirit, he cannot enter the kingdom of God. What is born of the flesh, is flesh; and what is born of the Spirit, is spirit. Marvel not that I say to you, you must be born anew. The wind blows where it will, and you hear its sound, but cannot tell whence it comes, nor whither it goes: so is every one born, who is born of the Spirit."

Nicodemus asked, "How can this be?" Jesus answered him, "Are you the teacher of Israel, and understand not this? Truly, truly, I say to you; we speak what we know, and testify of what we have seen; and you receive not our testimony. If I tell you earthly things, and you believe not, how will you believe should I tell you heavenly things? No one has ascended to heaven, but he that descended from heaven, —the Son of Man, who is in heaven. And as Moses lifted up the serpent in the wilderness, so must the Son of Man be lifted up; that whoever believes in him, may have eternal life.

"For God so loved the world, as to give his only begot-

The teacher of Israel. —Nicodemus was one of the Sanhedrim, and reference to him as *the* teacher implies that he was a prominent doctor. He came to Jesus by night to avoid observation; but Jesus told him at once that he must "be born of water" — must make an open profession of his belief in the new religion — if he would enter the kingdom of God. Thus early he announced his intention to organize a society, and the necessity of "confessing him before men."

ten Son, that whoever believes in him may not perish, but have eternal life. For God sent not his Son into the world to judge the world: but that through him the world may be saved. He who believes in him is not judged; but he who believes not is already judged, because he has not believed in the only begotten Son of God. And the ground of the judgment is, that light has come into the world, and men love darkness rather than the light, because their deeds are evil. For whoever does evil hates the light, and comes not to the light, lest his deeds should be exposed; but whoever does truth comes to the light, and it is made manifest, that his deeds are wrought in God."*

After this, Jesus and his disciples went into the country of Judea; and there remained and baptized, — though Jesus baptized not, but his disciples. And John also was baptizing in Ænon, near Salim, because there was an abundance of water there: and many came to him, and were baptized. For John was not yet cast into prison. Then there arose a question between some of John's disciples and a Jew about purification. And they went to John and said, "Rabbi, he who was with you beyond the Jordan, to whom you bore testimony, lo! he is baptizing, and all men resort to him." John answered, "A man can have nothing, but what is given him from heaven. You yourselves know that I said, I am not the Christ, but one sent before him.

Ænon.—This place was west of the Jordan, and about twenty miles north of Bethany, where Jesus was baptized. The river near this point is stated by Captain Lynch, to be about ten feet in depth.

* John iii. 1-21.

He who has the bride is the bridegroom: but the friend of the bridegroom, who stands by and hears him, rejoices greatly at the bridegroom's voice; this, then, my joy is fully attained."

"He must increase, but I must decrease. He who comes from above, is above all: he who is from the earth is earthly, and speaks earthly things. He who comes from heaven is above all. And what he has seen and heard, that he testifies and no man receives his testimony. But whoever receives his testimony attests his belief that God is true. He whom God has sent speaks the words of God; for God gives not the Spirit to him by measure. The Father loves the Son, and has committed all things into his hands. He who believes in the Son has eternal life: and he who believes not the Son, will not see life; but the wrath of God will abide on him."*

Now Herod the tetrarch, being reproved by John,

Herod the Tetrarch. — This was Antipas, a son of Herod the Great, who had died soon after the birth of Christ, leaving his kingdom to three sons. He was a weak, dissolute prince, and inherited all the vices of his father. Josephus relates that on a journey to Rome, he stopped at his brother Philip's house, and there, falling in love with Herodias, his brother's wife, determined to repudiate the daughter of Aretas, King of Petræa, whom he had married, and to marry Herodias. Herodias was a grand-daughter of Herod the Great, and had married his son Philip, whom his father had disinherited; and by him, had had one daughter — the Salome who danced before Antipas. She was a violent, ambitious woman, and dissatisfied with the obscure position of Philip, no doubt, entrapped Antipas into this alliance.

* John iii. 22-36.

for taking Herodias, his brother Philip's wife, and for all the evil he had done, laid hold on him, put him in chains, and cast him into prison; for John had said to Herod, "It is not lawful that you should have your brother's wife." Therefore Herodias was enraged against him, and would have killed him; but she could not: for Herod stood in awe of John, knowing that he was a just and holy man. He heard him gladly, doing many things at his suggestion; yet, for Herodias's sake, he would have put him to death, had he not feared the people, who regarded John as a prophet.*

Then, Jesus, hearing that John was cast into prison, left Judea and went again to Galilee; and his way lay through Samaria. And he came to a city of Samaria, called Sychar, near the field that Jacob gave

The wife of Antipas, discovering the project, fled to Machero, a strong fortress on the east of the Jordan, and in her father's dominions. A war between Aretas and Antipas followed, and Machero fell into the hands of the latter. There John was imprisoned, and subsequently beheaded. This incestuous marriage greatly scandalized the Jews, and in denouncing it, John only echoed the public opinion.

His way lay through Samaria. — The way through Samaria was the direct and usual route; but many travellers followed the more circuitous one to the east of the Jordan.

Samaria. — This country lay between Jerusalem and Galilee, and included the region bounded on the north by the range of hills which begins on the west at Mount Carmel, and runs east to the valley of the Jordan, and on the south, by the northern possessions of the tribe of Benjamin; and thus comprised the territory formerly occupied by the tribe

* Matt. iv. 12. xiv. 3-5. Mark vi. 17-20. Luke iii. 19-20. iv. 14.

to his son Joseph; and Jacob's well was there, and

of Ephraim, and the half-tribe of Manasseh. When the ten tribes were carried away captive to Babylon, the Assyrian King sent other nations to inhabit their country, and so Gentiles were placed "in the cities of Samaria, instead of the children of Israel." (2 Kings, xvii. 6, 23.) These people at first, worshipped idols; but being troubled with lions — because, as they supposed, they had not honored the God of the country — they asked the King of Assyria to send them one of the captive priests to teach them "how they should fear the Lord." The priest was sent, and henceforth they "feared the Lord, and served their graven images," — their religion becoming a mixture of idolatry and Judaism. When the Jews returned from Babylon, and began the rebuilding of the temple, the Samaritans offered their assistance; but the Jews rejected it on the ground of their idolatry and Assyrian descent. Then a bitter feeling arose between the two peoples, which was increased by certain renegade Jews who, from time to time, took refuge with the Samaritans. One of these renegades — Manasseh, a man of priestly lineage, who had been expelled from Jerusalem by Nehemiah for an unlawful marriage — about 409 B. C. obtained leave from the Persian King to build a temple on Mount Gerizim. The building of this temple increased the feud between the Jews and Samaritans, and many Jewish criminals and refugees from Justice being afterwards received and protected by the Samaritans, an irreconcilable hatred sprang up between the two nations. This continued till the time of Christ, when the Jews regarded the Samaritans as the worst of the human race, and had no dealings with them. Notwithstanding their Assyrian origin, the Samaritans claimed to be descended from Jacob (John 4. 12), and to have possession of the only authentic copy of the Pentateuch. They rejected the other Old Testament writings, and held that *Gerizim* had been designated by Moses as the place where "men should worship." The present people of Samaria are rude, insolent, and dangerous to strangers; and the former inhabitants, according to the prophets, were of quite as bad a character.

Being weary with his journey, Jesus sat down by the well: and it was about the hour of noon.

Sychar. — The true name of this place was Shechem, but Sychar — a Syriac word signifying a drunkard and a liar — was an opprobrious term applied to it by the Jews. It was forty miles north of Jerusalem, and fifty-two northwest from Jericho, and one of the oldest and most populous cities of Palestine. It received the name of Neapolis from Vespasian, and on coins still extant is called Flavia Neapolis. Its present name, Naplous, is an Arabic corruption of Neapolis. It is situated in a narrow valley between Mount Gerizim on the south, and Ebal on the north, and its environs are described as being surpassingly beautiful. Gerizim rises eight hundred feet above the town, and a lofty range of mountains bounds its horizon on all sides. Streams, issuing from numerous springs, flow down the mountain slopes, spreading verdure and fertility in every direction. Dr. Robinson says, "the whole valley is filled with gardens of vegetables, and orchards of all kinds of fruits, watered by fountains. It burst upon us like a scene of fairy enchantment. We saw nothing to compare with it in all Palestine." The streets of the city are narrow, and vaulted over, and mulberry, orange, and pomegranate-trees grow in among the houses, and load the air with perfume. The gardens are the homes of numerous nightingales, and other birds, and from them, the valley takes the name of "the musical vale of Palestine." The city has now a population of about two thousand, only two hundred of whom are Samaritans.

Jacob's well — is located about a mile and a half east from Naplous, at the foot of Mount Gerizim, and near a wretched hamlet, called Balâta. It is excavated in the solid limestone rock, is perfectly round, with sides hewn smooth and regular, and is nine feet in diameter by about eighty in depth. Formerly the opening was vaulted over in a small chamber under the surface of the ground, and surrounded by a terrace of rude masonry — on which, probably, Jesus sat — but this is now fallen in, and nothing can be seen below, but a

Then a woman of Samaria coming to the well to draw water, Jesus said to her, "Give me to drink;" — for his disciples had gone away to the city to buy food. The woman said to him, "How is it that you who are a Jew, ask drink of me, who am a woman of Samaria? (for the Jews have no dealing with the Samaritans.") Jesus answered her, "Had you known the gift of God, and who it is that says to you, 'Give me to drink;' you would have asked of him, and he would have given you living water." The woman said to him, "Sir, you have no bucket to draw with, and the

shallow pit nearly filled with stones and rubbish. There is no mention of this well in the Old Testament, and it may have received its name only from the fact of being near the field which Jacob gave to his son Joseph. In this field, a quarter of a mile to the north of the well, is "the tomb of Joseph." This is a small square enclosure, with whitewashed walls, surmounted by a dome. A rough pillar, black with fire, is at its head, and another at its foot, and on the walls are two slabs with Hebrew inscriptions. There is no doubt that this is the resting-place of the bones of the Patriarch.

Being weary. — How far Jesus had journeyed that day, we do not know, but the fact that he was too weary to go on, while his disciples could walk three miles, — a mile and a half and back, — before taking rest or food, shows that he must have had a more than ordinarily delicate physical constitution. This is also shown by his inability to bear his cross, and by his surviving the torture of crucifixion only a few hours when ordinary natures often endured it for two or three days.

A woman. — It was the custom of the country for women to work in the fields, and this woman was probably thus employed in the neighborhood of the well.

No bucket. — The original word seems to require this rendering. Wells in the east are not furnished with drawing

7

well is deep: whence then have you the living water? Are you greater than our father Jacob, who gave us this well, and drank of it himself, and his children, and his cattle?" Jesus answered her, "Whoever drinks of this water will thirst again: but whoever drinks of the water I will give him, will never thirst; but the water that I will give him will be in him a well of water springing up into eternal life." The woman said to him, "Sir, give me this water, that I may not thirst nor come here to draw." Jesus said to her, "Go, call your husband, and come hither." The woman answered, "I have no husband." Jesus said, "You say well, I have no husband; for though you have had five husbands, he whom you now have is not your husband: in that you speak truly." The woman said to him, "Sir, I perceive you are a prophet. Our fathers worshipped on this mountain; but you Jews say, that the place where men ought to worship is in Jerusalem." Jesus said to her, "Woman, believe me, the hour is coming when neither on this mountain, nor yet at Jerusalem, will men worship the Father. You worship, you know not what: we know what we worship; for salvation is of the Jews. But the hour is coming, and now is, when the true worshippers will worship the Father in spirit and in truth; for the Father seeks such worship. God is a Spirit: and those that worship him must worship in

apparatus, and travellers provide themselves with small leathern buckets, which they carry on their journeys.

On this mountain. — Mount Gerizim on which was the temple. The original edifice was destroyed by John Hyrcanus, 131, B. C. but it had probably been rebuilt, though with less magnificence.

spirit and in truth." The woman said to him, "I know that the Messiah is coming, — when he comes, he will tell us all things." Jesus said to her, "I who speak to you am he."

And upon this his disciples came and wondered that he was talking with a woman; yet no one said, "What seek you? or, why talk you with her?" The woman then left her waterpot, and going away to the city, said to the men, "Come, see a man who has told me all things that ever I did. Is not he the Christ?" Then they came from the city to meet him. In the mean time his disciples prayed him, saying, "Master eat." But he said to them, "I have food to eat that you know not of." Then they said one to another, "Has any one brought him aught to eat?" Jesus said to them, "My food is to do the will of him that sent me, and to finish his work. Say you not, 'After four months comes the harvest?' Lo! I say to you, lift up your eyes, and look on the fields; for they are already white for the harvest. And he who reaps receives wages, and gathers fruit to life eternal: that both the sower and the reaper may rejoice together. In this is fulfilled that true saying; 'One sows, and another reaps.' I send you to reap where you have not labored: others have labored, and you have come into their labors."

Talking with a woman. — It was considered by the Jews highly indecorous to converse with women in public, and the Rabbis held that to discourse with them on any important or serious subject, was unsuited to the dignity of a doctor of the law. It is Christianity alone, which has elevated woman to her true position as the equal of man.

Four months. — No doubt a Jewish proverb, that time being the usual interval between seed-time and harvest.

And many of the Samaritans of the city believed in him on the testimony of the woman, that he had told her all that she ever did. So when they came to him, they besought him to abide with them: and he remained there two days. And many more believed because of his own teaching; and said to the woman, "No longer do we believe because of your words; for we ourselves have heard him and know that this is truly the Saviour of the world."*

After two days he departed thence, and went to Galilee, though he himself testified that a prophet has no honor in his own country.

But when he came to Galilee, the Galileans welcomed him, having seen all that he did at Jerusalem during the festival; for they also went to the passover. So he came again to Cana in Galilee, where he made the water wine. And there was a certain officer of the court whose son was sick at Capernaum. He, hearing that Jesus had come from Judea into Galilee, came to him, and besought him to go down and heal his son, who lay at the point of death. Then said Jesus, "Can you not believe, without seeing signs and wonders?"

Officer of the court.—The court of Herod Antipas. He seems to have had his usual residence at Capernaum, and it is not an improbable supposition, that he was Chusa, Herod's steward, whose wife afterwards attended on Jesus.

Capernaum—was at the northwest extremity of the sea of Gennesaret, and distant about a day's journey from Cana. It was *down* from Cana, the latter place being located in the hilly region at the southwest of Capernaum.

Can you not believe.—The *you* in the original is in the plural, which indicates that this remark was addressed not so

* John 4: 3-42.

And the king's officer said to him," Master, come down before my child die." Jesus said to him, "Go your way; your son lives." And the man believed what Jesus told him, and went his way. And while he was going down, his servants met him, and told him that his son was well. Then he inquired of them the hour when he began to amend; and they said, "Yesterday, at the seventh hour, the fever left him." Then the father knew that it was the same hour when Jesus said to him, "Your son lives," and he believed, and all his household. This was the second miracle that Jesus wrought in Galilee, after coming from Judea,* and his fame spread abroad through all that region.

From that time Jesus began to preach, and to teach in the Synagogues, saying, "The time is fulfilled. The

much to the officer, who showed a becoming faith, as to others who were standing about Jesus.

The Synagogue. — The word means congregation, or house of gathering: and was used to denote the local places of worship, of which there were one or more in nearly every town of Judea and Galilee. In Jerusalem, according to Josephus, there were four hundred and eighty. They were of very remote antiquity, and were the principal means of keeping the religion of their fathers alive among the Jews. The building was erected on the model of the temple, with a central structure, surrounded by a court, and supported by pillars, and it varied in size with the population of the locality. It always stood on the highest ground, in or near the town to which it belonged, and was so constructed that the people on entering, and when standing up for prayers, had their faces toward Jerusalem. It was commonly built at the cost of the district; but sometimes was erected by a rich Jew, or a friendly prose-

* John 4: 43-54.

kingdom of God is at hand. Repent and believe the gospel." And he was glorified of all.*

And going to Nazareth, where he was brought up, he went, as was his custom, into the Synagogue on the

lyte, (Luke xii. 5). Its internal arrangement was copied after the tabernacle. At the upper, or Jerusalem end, was the ark, a chest containing the sacred book, and here were the "uppermost seats" (Matt. xxiii. 6.) so much desired by the Pharisees. The people sat around, facing the pulpit, which was farther towards the centre of the building, on a raised platform, upon which several persons could stand at once. At this pulpit the Reader stood to read the Scriptures, or sat down to teach. The congregation were divided, the men on one side, the women on the other, a low partition, four or five feet high, running between them. In small towns there was often only one Rabbi, or teacher; but in larger places there was a college of Elders, (Luke vii. 3,) presided over by "the Chief of the Synagogue." (Luke viii. 41. 49. Acts xviii. 8. -17.) The prominent officer in the larger Synagogues was known as the officiating minister, and he read the prayers in the name of the people; but the minister referred to in the text, was a subordinate officer, employed to open the doors and prepare the building for service. Forms of prayer were used in the worship, (Luke xi. 1,) and the books of Moses, and the Prophets were read every Sabbath, portions being read consecutively, and the whole being gone through every third year. These were followed by the sermon, or exposition from the Rabbi. The officers of the Synagogue exercised in certain cases, judicial power. (Matt. x. 17. Mark xiii. 9.) They did not, however, descend to the trivial disputes of daily life, but attended to the graver offences against religion and morals. See, for a fuller account of the Synagogue, *Smith's Bible Dictionary*.

As his custom was.—In the beginning of his ministry Jesus spoke in the Synagogues, but when his fame had spread

* Matt. ix. 17. Mark i. 14, 15. Luke iv. 14. 15.

Sabbath, and stood up to read. And the book of the prophet Isaiah being given to him, he unrolled it, and found the place where it is written: "The Spirit of the Lord is upon me. He has anointed me to preach glad tidings to the poor; he has sent me to heal the broken hearted, to proclaim deliverance to the captives, the recovery of sight to the blind, to set at liberty the oppressed, to proclaim the joyful year of the Lord." And rolling up the volume he gave it to the minister, and sat down; and the eyes of all in the Synagogue were fastened on him. Then he said to them, "To-day this scripture is fulfilled in your ears." And all wondered, and bore testimony to the gracious words which came from his mouth. But they said, "Is not this the son of Joseph?" And he said to them, "You will surely say to me this proverb, 'Physician, heal thyself: what we have heard of your doing in Capernaum, do also here in your own country.' But I say to you, No prophet is accepted in his own country; and I tell you in truth, that many widows were in Israel in the days of Elijah, when the heaven was shut up three years and six months, when great famine was in all the land; but to none of them was Elijah sent, but to a widow of Zarephath, a city of Sidon. And many lepers were in Israel in the time of Elisha the prophet; yet none of them was

abroad, and multitudes flocked to him, he taught in the open air, by the sea-side, on the mountains, and even in desert places.

The book of Isaiah.—Books among the ancients were written on strips of vellum, or parchment, rolled together on two rollers, beginning at each end. Jesus read from Isaiah lxi. 1. 2.

cleansed but Naaman the Syrian." And all in the Synagogue, on hearing this, were filled with anger, and rising up, they thrust him out of the town, and led him to the brow of the hill whereon the town is built, to cast him down headlong. But he, passing through the midst of them, went his way down to Capernaum, and taught there on the Sabbath days. And

The brow of the hill. — The place at which tradition locates this scene is a rocky precipice about two miles from Nazareth. There is, however, another declivity within the town, not far from the supposed site of the Synagogue, down which Jesus might have been "cast headlong."

Capernaum. — This town afterwards became the residence of Jesus, and is one of the few places whose destruction he predicted (Matt. xi. 23. Luke x. 15). The prediction has been so perfectly fulfilled, that now even its site is with difficulty determined. The probability is that it was at the north-western extremity of the lake, at the locality now occupied by Tell Hum — which is nothing more than a shapeless mass of ruins, usually deserted, but tenanted, now and then, by a few wandering Bedâwins. There are at this place evident remains of a large town, and its surroundings accord with a description given by Josephus. The ruins are piled up in wild confusion for half a mile along the shore of the lake, and extend back a quarter of a mile to a neighboring hill. The houses were built of basalt, quite black, rudely cut, and so compact that the stones may yet remain for thousands of years. Among them are the ruins of what is supposed to have been a Synagogue, of beautiful marble, with columns, entablatures, and cornices cut in the highest style of art. Everything about the ruins grows luxuriantly, and the town must once have been the centre of a most fertile region. From Josephus it is certain that Capernaum was in a rich, busy district, and on the western shore of the lake — which in the time of Christ, was one of the most prosperous and populous districts of Palestine. While Jesus was brought up at Naza-

they were astonished at his teaching; for he spoke with power. Now Capernaum is on the sea coast, in the borders of Zabulon and Nephthalim; and thus were fulfilled the words of Isaiah the prophet, "The land of Zabulon, and the land of Nephthalim, by the way of the sea, Galilee of the Gentiles. The people who sat in darkness have seen a great light, and to those in the region and shadow of death, light is sprung up.*

And as the people pressed upon him to hear the word of God, he stood by the lake of Gennesaret,

reth, this was his "own city." Here he frequently taught in the Synagogue built by the Centurion, and here, he called Matthew, and performed many of his most wonderful works.

Zebulon and Nepthalim. — Two of the ten tribes.

Galilee of the Gentiles, — was Upper Galilee — the region about Tyre and Sidon, and was so called because principally occupied by Gentiles.

Lake of Gennesaret. — Most of the public life of Jesus was passed on the borders of this lake, then in the most densely populated region of Palestine; no less than nine cities standing on its very shores. It is of oval form, about thirteen miles long, and six broad. The river Jordan enters at its northern end, and passes out at the southern. In fact the bed of the lake is only a lower section of the great Jordan valley. It is seven hundred feet below the level of the ocean, and its great depression makes the climate of its shores almost tropical. In summer the heat is intense, and even in early spring the air has the balminess of Egypt. The water of the lake is sweet, cool and transparent, and as the beach is everywhere pebbly, it has a beautiful sparkling look. It abounds in fish now, as in ancient times. The scenery around is bleak and picturesque; and the environs are rich in natural beauty. Josephus describes the region as in his time a perfect

* Luke iv: 16-32. Matt. iv: 13-16.

and saw two boats moored by the shore; but the fishermen had gone out of them, and were washing their nets. Entering one of the boats, which was Simon's, he prayed him to push out a little from the land, and then sitting down, he taught the multitude from the boat. When he had finished speaking, he said to Simon, "Launch out now into deep water, and let down your net for a draught;" and Simon answered: "Master, we have toiled all the night, and taken nothing; but at your word I will let down the net." And doing so they enclosed a vast number of fishes, so that their nets were nigh bursting, and they made signs to their partners, in the other boat to come and help them. They came, and filled both the boats, so as almost to sink them. And Simon Peter seeing this, fell down at the knees of Jesus, saying, "Depart from me; for I am a sinful man, O Lord;" for he, and all

paradise, where vines and all manner of fruits grew most luxuriantly, and at all seasons of the year.

Two boats. — These were, no doubt, such small boats as are now used in fishing on smooth, flat beaches. In fishing one end of the net is attached to the shore; the fishermen then row out and return, dropping the net as they go, and making a sort of semicircle from the shore, and as the net is sunk with weights to the bottom, and floated with corks at the top; all the fish in that compass are included, and drawn to the shore. Josephus says there were two hundred and thirty of these boats on the lake, each manned by four or five men.

Taught from the boat. — In the vicinity of Tell Hum — the supposed site of Capernaum — are numerous inlets, where a boat could ride in safety within a few feet of the shore, while a multitude, seated on both sides, around, and in front of the boat, could hear readily.

Depart from me. — It was a superstition among the Jews

that were with him were amazed at the draught of fishes they had taken. And so too, were James and John the sons of Zebedee, who were partners with Simon. But Jesus said to them, "Fear not: follow me, and I will make you fishers of men." And having brought the boat to land, they left all, and followed him, and James the son of Zebedee, and John his brother, leaving their father in his boat with the hired servants, also went after him.*

And going again into Capernaum, he entered the Synagogue on the Sabbath and taught. And all were astonished at his teaching: for he spoke as one having authority, and not as the Scribes. And in the Synagogue was a man possessed by a foul spirit; who cried out with a loud voice: "Let us alone; why dost thou trouble us, thou Jesus of Nazareth? Hast thou come to destroy us? I know thee who thou art,—the Holy One of God." And Jesus rebuked the foul spirit, saying, "Hold thy peace, and come out of the man." And when the spirit had torn the man, and thrown him in the midst, he cried with a loud voice, and came out of him. And all were amazed, so much so, that they said to one another, "What is this? what new teaching is this? for with authority he commands even the foul spirits, and they obey him." And immediately his fame spread abroad through all the region round about Galilee.†

that he who had seen a remarkable manifestation of God, would surely die. The word rendered amazed denotes that Peter was not merely astonished, but struck with terror.

* Matt. iv: 18-22. Mark 1: 16-20. Luke v: 1-10.
† Mark i. 21-28. Luke iv. 31-37.

As soon as they came out of the Synagogue, he entered the house of Simon and Andrew, with James and John. Now Simon's wife's mother lay sick of a fever, and immediately they told him of her; and going to her, he took her by the hand, and lifting her up, rebuked the fever, and it left her at once, so that she arose and ministered to them. And at even when the sun was setting, all the city gathered together at the door, and they brought to him all who were diseased, and those who were possessed with demons. and he cast out the spirits with a word, forbidding them to speak, because they knew him. But they cried out, saying, "Thou art the Christ, the Son of God." He also laid his hands on those who were sick with divers diseases, and healed them. And in the morning, rising a long time before day, he went out to a solitary place, and there prayed. And Simon and others followed, and when they found him, said to him, "All men seek for you," and they prayed him not to depart from them. But he said to them, "I must go to the neighboring towns, and preach the kingdom of God there also: for therefore came I forth."*

And he went about all Galilee, teaching in the Synagogues, and preaching the glad tidings of the kingdom, and casting out demons, and healing all kinds of diseases among the people. And his fame spread throughout all Syria; and great multitudes followed

Sick of a fever.—Tell Hum is environed with marshes which now breed fevers of a very violent and fatal character.

* Matt. viii. 14-17. Mark i. 29-39. Luke iv. 38-44.

him from Galilee, and Decapolis, and from Jerusalem, and Judea, and from beyond the Jordan.*

And when he was in a certain city, a man full of leprosy, seeing him, came, and kneeling down before him, said, "Lord, if thou wilt, thou canst make me clean." And Jesus, moved with pity, stretched forth his hand and touched him, saying, "I will: be thou clean;" and as soon as he had spoken, the leprosy left the man, and he was cleansed. Sending him away immediately, Jesus charged him strictly to tell no one, but to go, show himself to a priest, and make the offering which Moses had directed, for a

Leprosy. — This is a troublesome, and, in its advanced stages, an incurable disease. It is of three kinds, the white, black, and red leprosy. Its first appearance is in spots on the skin, but it is deeply seated in the joints and bones, and, when considerably advanced, produces acute suffering. An observer describes it as follows: — "Its commencement is imperceptible. There appear only some few spots on the skin. At first they are attended with no pain or inconvenience; but no means whatever will remove them. The disease imperceptibly increases for many years. The spots become large, and spread over the whole body. When the disease advances the upper part of the nose swells, the nostrils become enlarged, and the nose itself soft. Tumors appear on the jaws; the eyebrows swell; the ears become thick; the points of the fingers, as also the feet and the toes swell; the nails become scaly; the joints and the hands separate and drop off. In the last stage of the disease, the patient becomes a hideous spectacle, and *falls to pieces.*" Leprosy is highly contagious, and by the Jewish law the leper was forbidden to eat with others, and obliged to dwell outside the towns, apart by himself.

The offering — here referred to, was two doves, one of which was sacrificed, the other allowed to go free.

* Matt. iv. 23-25.

proof to the people; but the man went out, and began to blaze the matter abroad, so much so, that great multitudes came to Jesus, to hear and be healed, and he could no longer enter openly into the towns, but remained without in solitary places. There people came to him from every quarter; but he withdrew from them, and going into the desert, prayed.*

And after some days, he again entered his own town, —Capernaum; and as soon as it was noised abroad that he was in the house, many people gathered together, so many that there was no room to receive them, not even about the door: and he preached the word to them. And as he was teaching, Pharisees and teachers of the law were sitting by, who had come from every town of Galilee, and from Judea, and Jerusalem: and the power of the Lord was present to heal the people. And they came bringing one sick of the palsy, borne of four; and sought means to take him in, and lay him before Jesus. But as they could not come near him, on account of the throng, they broke up the roof where he was: and going upon the house-top, let

Palsy. — A paralytic disease of different degrees of intensity. In its worst forms, which are common in the east, the patient loses all control of his limbs, suffers excruciating torture, and soon dies.

Uncovered the roof. — Houses at the east are built about a court, and with flat roofs, which are usually approached by a stairway leading up from the street. The roof of these courts is supported on joists, about three feet apart; and over them is spread a covering of short sticks, placed closely together, and cemented with mortar. Owing to the crowd, Jesus, no doubt, stood in the court of the house, and it, therefore, was

* Matt. viii. 2-4. Mark i. 40-45. Luke v. 12-16.

down the bed whereon the sick man lay, through the tiling, into the midst before Jesus. He, seeing their faith, said to the sick of the palsy, "Son, be of good cheer; your sins are forgiven you." And certain of the doctors said to themselves, "This man blasphemes! Who can forgive sins but God only?" Jesus knowing their thoughts, said to them, "Why think you evil in your hearts? Which is easier to say, 'Your sins are forgiven,' or to say, 'Arise, and walk.' But that you may know the Son of Man has power on earth to forgive sins, (then he said to the sick of the palsy,) Arise, take up your bed, and go to your own house." And the sick man rose at once, took up his bed, and went forth before them all; and they were all amazed, saying, "We have seen strange things to-day," and they glorified God, who had given such power to men.*

And he went forth again by the sea-side, and great multitudes resorted to him, and he taught them. And as he passed along, he saw Matthew, the son of Alpheus sitting at the receipt of custom, and he said to him, "Follow me." And he rose up, left all, and followed him.†

easy to uncover the roof, and let down the paralytic "into the midst before him."

*Mark ii. 1-12. Luke v. 17-26.

† Matt. ix. 9. Mark ii. 13-14. Luke v. 27-28.

PART FOURTH.

THE SECOND PASSOVER, AND SUBSEQUENT EVENTS.

TIME — ONE YEAR.

LIFE OF JESUS.

PART FOURTH.

AFTER this, there was a festival of the Jews; and Jesus went up to Jerusalem. Now at Jerusalem near the sheep gate, is a pool, called in Hebrew Bethesda, having five porches; and in these lay a great

This *Festival* is supposed to have been the Passover.

Sheep Gate. — The word *market* is not in the original. This was no doubt the sheep gate mentioned by Nehemiah, (iii. 1–32, and xii. 39), and was probably near the Temple, for greater convenience in conveying the sacrifices into the sacred building. The place which tradition locates as the pool of Bethesda, is a little to the northeast of the ancient site of the Temple, and Maundrell (1697) describes it as "about one hundred and twenty paces long, forty broad, and at least eight deep; with at one end, the remains of three or four arches which are regarded as the ruins of the five porches, in which lay the blind, halt, and withered." In the time of Sandys (1611,) the spring which fed the pool was running; but Maundrell says it was dry when he saw it; and more recent travellers describe the pool as now destitute of water. It is supposed that the spring, which formerly filtered through the rocks, has become dammed up by the ruins and rubbish. Eusebius describes the pool existing in his time as being in two compartments; one supplied by rains, the other, by a spring, and the water of the latter as of a reddish hue, owing,

number of sick people, — blind, halt, and withered. And a certain man was there who had been infirm thirty and eight years. Seeing him lying there, and knowing that he had been a long time in that condition, Jesus said to him, "Would you be made well?" The infirm man answered, "Sir, I have no one to put me into the pool when the water is troubled; but, while I am going, another gets down before me." Jesus said to him, "Rise, take up your bed, and walk." And immediately the man was made well, and took up his bed, and walked: and the day was the Sabbath.

The Jews, therefore, said to the man who was cured, "It is the Sabbath: it is not lawful for you to carry your bed." He answered them, "He who made me well, said to me, "Take up your bed and walk." Then they asked, "Who is the man who said to you, 'Take up your bed and walk?'" But he that was cured knew not who it was; for a throng was in the place, and Jesus had withdrawn himself. Afterward

as tradition then affirmed, to the fact that the flesh of sacrifices was once washed in it before offering. The Bourdeaux Pilgrim (A. D., 333), confirms this statement of Eusebius. The name Bethesda, — which denotes "house of mercy," — gives color to the supposition that the pool had medicinal virtues; but whether they were owing to the mineral qualities of the water, or, as some suppose, to its impregnation with the blood of the sacrificed animals, it is impossible to determine. The clause in the common version referring to an angel "troubling the water," is not in the oldest MSS. It was probably a Jewish superstition which, from being originally inserted as a note in the margin, finally crept into the text of some of the more recent copies.

It is not lawful to carry your bed. — The Jews were forbidden to carry burdens on the Sabbath. See Jer. xxii, 21, and Neh. xiii. 15.

Jesus found him in the temple, and said to him, "Lo! you are well: sin no more, lest something worse befall you." The man went away and told the Jews that it was Jesus who had made him well. And upon this the Jews went in pursuit of Jesus, because he had done thus on the Sabbath. But Jesus said to them, "My Father is always working, and so also I work." For this reason the Jews were the more bent on killing him, because he not only had broken the Sabbath, but also had said that God was his Father, thus making himself equal with God. Then Jesus said to them "Truly, truly, I tell you, The Son can do nothing of himself, but what he sees the Father do; but whatever he does, the Son also does in like manner. For the Father loves the Son, and shows him all that he does: and greater works than these will he show him, that you may wonder. For as the Father raises the dead, and gives them life, so also the Son gives life to whom he will. And the Father condemns no man, but has committed all condemnation to the Son: that all should honor the Son, even as they honor the Father. He who honors not the Son, honors not the Father who sent him.

"Truly, truly, I tell you, He who hears my words, and believes him who sent me, has eternal life, and comes not into judgment; but has passed from death to life. Truly, truly, I tell you, the hour is coming, and now is, when the dead shall hear the voice of the Son of God; and those that hear it shall live. For as the Father has life in himself, so has he given to the Son to have life in himself; and he has given him authority to pass judgment also, because he is a son of man. Wonder not at this; for the hour is coming, when all who are in the graves shall hear his voice, and come forth; those who have done good, to the resurrection of life; and those who have done evil, to the resurrection of judgment. Of myself I can do nothing: as I hear, I judge: and my judgment is just; because I seek not my own will, but the will of him who sent me.

"You say, 'If I testify of myself, my testimony is not true.' There is another who bears testimony of me; and I know that his testimony of me is true. You have sent to John, and he has testified to the truth. I receive not testimony from man; but I say this that you may be saved. He was a lamp burning and shining; and for a time you were willing to rejoice in his light. But I have greater testimony than John's; for the works which the Father has given me to do, — these works that I am doing, they testify that the Father has sent me; and thus the Father who sent me, has himself borne testimony of me. You have never heard his voice nor seen his form; and his word is not abiding in you; for you believe not him whom he has sent. You search the Scriptures, because you think that in them you

Because he is a son of man. — The definite article is wanting in the original. Paul expresses the same idea. "For we have not a high priest who cannot be touched with a feeling of our infirmities; but one who was tried in all points as we are, yet without sin."

You say, if I testify of myself. — The words "you say" are supplied. The context requires us to suppose that Jesus is repeating a remark of the Pharisees.

have eternal life,—they are my witnesses, and yet you will not come to me to have life.

I desire not glory from men. But I know you, that you have not the love of God in you. I have come in my Father's name, and you receive me not; should another come in his own name, him you will receive. How can you believe, who desire honor of one another, and seek not the honor that comes from Him, the only God. Think not that I shall accuse you to the Father: there is one who accuses you,—Moses, in whom you trust. But if you had faith in Moses, you would have faith in me; for he wrote of me. But if you believe not his writings, how should you believe my words?*

On the second Sabbath after the first, Jesus was passing through a field of grain, and his disciples being hungry, plucked the ears of grain as they went along, and ate them, rubbing them in their hands. But some of the Pharisees observing this, said to him, "Lo! your disciples are doing what the

On the second Sabbath after the first.—This clause has given great perplexity to commentators. It probably should read "The second Sabbath after the first day of unleavened bread." This was near the barley harvest, when the ears would be ripe. The Jews were not allowed to eat on the Sabbath before they had attended the services of the Synagogue. This may explain the hunger of the disciples. From Deut. xxiii. 25, it will be seen that the Jew was permitted to pluck and eat the standing grain of his neighbor. Dr. Thomson says in regard to this custom, "I have often seen my muleteers, as we passed along the wheat fields, pluck off ears, rub them in their hands, and eat them unroasted, just as the disciples are said to have done."

*John v. 1-47.

Law forbids on the Sabbath." Jesus answered, "Have you not read what David did, when he and those with him were hungry. How he entered the house of God, in the time of Abiathar, the chief priest, and ate the shew-bread, which was not lawful for him to do nor for those with him, but only for the priests? Or have you not read in the Law how on the Sabbath days the priests in the temple break the Sabbath and are blameless? Now I tell you, that one greater than the temple is here. But had you known what this means, 'I desire mercy, and not sacrifices,' you would not have condemned the guiltless. The Sabbath was made for man, not man for the Sabbath: so that the Son of Man is Lord even of the Sabbath."*

What the law forbids on the Sabbath. — The Jews were so scrupulous in regard to the observance of the Sabbath, that in their wars with Antiochus and the Romans, they did not defend themselves on that day. This Pompey discovered, and thus he took Jerusalem. The Mosaic law says, (Ex. xxxi. 14: xxxv. 2.) "Whoever does any work on the Sabbath shall surely be put to death." "Ye shall kindle no fire throughout your buildings on the Sabbath" (Ex. xxxv. 3.) In Numbers xv. 32–36, a man is found gathering sticks on the Sabbath, "and the Lord said to Moses, 'This man shall surely be put to death: the whole congregation shall stone him with stones without the camp.'" Therefore, in every one of the numerous instances in which Jesus disregarded this law, he hazarded his life.

Abiathar was chief, not high priest. — When David ate the shew-bread, Ahimelech, his father, was high priest, but he was soon after slain and then Abiathar succeeded to the office.

I desire mercy and not sacrifices. — See Hosea vi, 6.

*Matt. xii. 1–8. Mark ii. 23–28. Luke vi. 1–5.

Departing thence, he went on another Sabbath into the Synagogue, and taught; and a man was there whose right hand was withered. Now the Scribes and Pharisees were watching to see if he would cure the man on the Sabbath; that they might find an accusation against him. And they asked him, "Is it lawful to heal on the Sabbath?" But he knew their thoughts, and said to the man, "Rise, and stand up in the midst." And he arose and stood up. Then Jesus said to them, "I will ask you a question. Is it lawful on the Sabbath to do good, or to do evil? to save life, or to destroy it? What man among you, who owns a sheep, will not, if it fall into a pit on the Sabbath, lay hold of it and lift it out? Is not a man of more worth than a sheep? It is lawful, then, to do good on the Sabbath." They could say nothing, and looking round upon them with indignation, being grieved for their hardness of heart, he said to the man, "Stretch forth your hand." And he stretched it forth; and it was restored, sound as the other. Then the Pharisees were filled with madness, and going out, concerted with one another, and with the Herodians,

The Synagogue. — From the definite manner in which this Synagogue is spoken of, it is supposed that the one at Capernaum is referred to. In the same definite way the house — probably Peter's, — which Jesus occupied at Capernaum is often alluded to.

Withered Hand. — Such a rigidity of the nerves and muscles as unfitted the limb for use, was what the Jews understood as "withered."

To save life or to destroy it. — As the Pharisees were then plotting to entrap Jesus into a breach of the Sabbath, so as to take his life, there was peculiar force in this question.

how to destroy him.* But Jesus knowing it, withdrew with his disciples to the sea; and great numbers from Galilee and Judea, and Jerusalem, and Idumea, and beyond the Jordan, and from about Tyre and Sidon, hearing what great works he had done, followed him, and he healed them all. And he directed his disciples to have a small boat in waiting, lest the people should throng him; for he had healed many; so that all who were diseased crowded round to touch him: and foul spirits, also fell down before him, crying out: "Thou art the Son of God." But he strictly charged them not to make him known. And thus was fulfilled what had been written by Isaiah the prophet, "Behold my servant whom I have chosen, my beloved with whom I am well pleased; I will put my Spirit upon him, and he will declare my law to the Gentiles. He will not strive, nor cry aloud; neither will his voice be heard in the streets. A bruised reed he will not break, and smoking flax he will not quench, till he sends forth truth to victory. And in him will the nations trust."†

And going up into a mountain, he continued all night in prayer to God. And when it was day, he called to him his disciples, and of their num-

From Judea, etc. — The previous multitudes who had followed Jesus, had been Galileans, therefore the people from the other provinces are now separately mentioned.

Smoking Flax. — The wicks of lamps were of flax, and when the oil was well nigh exhausted, the flax would naturally smoke.

* Matt. xii. 9-14. Mark iii. 1-6. Luke vi. 6-11.
† Matt. xii. 15, 21. Mark iii. 7-12.

ber chose twelve, whom he also named Apostles, to be with him, and to go forth to preach, and to have power to heal sicknesses, and to cast out demons.

The names of the twelve Apostles were these: First, Simon, whom he called Peter; then Andrew his brother; James the son of Zebedee, and John his brother, whom he surnamed Boanerges, (that is, The sons of thunder:) Philip and Bartholomew, Thomas and Matthew, the tax gatherer: James the son of Alpheus, and Lebbeus, also called Thaddeus; Simon the Zealot, and Judas Iscariot, — he who betrayed him. And coming down with them, he stood in the plain, where were many of his disciples, and a great number of people from all Judea and Jerusalem, and from the sea-coast of Tyre and Sidon, who had come to hear him, and to be healed of their diseases and of foul spirits; and the whole multitude sought to touch him, for power went out of him, and cured them all.*

Seeing the multitude, he went up on the mountain

The Zealots, were a class of fanatics who took upon themselves to enforce a rigid observance of the ceremonial law.

The Mountain. — The definite article is again used in the original in referring to this mountain, which must have been an eminence near Capernaum. Maundrell says that "a few points to the north (of Mount Tabor) appears what is called the Mount of the Beatitudes, — a small rising, from which our blessed Lord delivered his sermon in v. vi. vii. chapters of Matthew. Not far from this little hill, is the city Saphat, supposed to be the ancient Bethulia. It stands upon a very eminent and commanding mountain, glistening with a noble

*Matt. x. 2-4. Mark iii. 13-19. Luke vi. 12-19.

and sat down; and his disciples coming to him, he taught them, saying:

Blessed are the poor in spirit, for theirs is the kingdom of heaven.

Blessed are those that mourn, for they will be comforted.

Blessed are the meek, for they will inherit the land.

Blessed are those who hunger and thirst for righteousness, for they will be filled.

Blessed are the merciful, for they will receive mercy.

Blessed are the pure in heart, for they will see God.

Blessed are the peace-makers, for they will be the children of God.

Blessed are they who are persecuted for righteousness' sake, for theirs is the kingdom of heaven.

Blessed are you when men revile you, and persecute you, and say all manner of evil against you, falsely, for my sake. Rejoice, and leap for joy, for great is your reward in heaven: So their fathers persecuted the prophets who were before you.

But alas for you who are rich! for you have your consolation.

Alas for you who are full! for you will hunger.

Alas for you who laugh now! for you will mourn and weep.

Alas for you, when all men speak well of you! for so their fathers did of the false prophets.

You are the salt of the earth; but if the salt lose its

castle, and is seen far and near, — seeming to command the whole country round to a great distance." To this city Jesus is supposed to have pointed, when he referred to the city set on a hill.

The Salt of Palestine is obtained from marshes along the

savor, with what shall it be salted? It is then good for nothing; but is cast out, and trodden under foot of men.

You are the light of the world. A city set on a hill cannot be hid. Nor do men light a lamp to put it under a bushel, but on a stand; that it may give light to all in the house. So let your light shine before men; that they may see your good deeds, and glorify your Father in heaven.

Think not that I have come to annul the Law, or the

sea shore, or from salt lakes in the interior, which dry up in summer. By the evaporation of the water the marshes are left covered with a thick crust of saline material, which is afterwards gathered into heaps, like hay-cocks in a meadow. Dr. Thomson relates that he found the large winter lake, southeast of Aleppo, dried up in the end of August, and the entire basin, as far as the eye could reach, as white as snow, from an incrustation of course salt. Maundrell says, that he found at Jebbul, salt which had entirely "lost its savor," and Dr. Thomson found the same in localities at the south end of the Dead Sea. He says, "it is a well known fact that the salt of this country, (Palestine), when in contact with the ground, or exposed to rain and sun, does become insipid and useless. From the manner in which it is gathered, much earth and other impurities are necessarily collected with it. Not a little of it is so impure that it cannot be used at all, and such salt soon effloresces, and turns to dust, — not to fruitful soil, however. It is not only good for nothing itself, but it actually destroys all fertility wherever it is thrown; and this is the reason why it is cast into the street. There is no place about the house, yard or garden, where it can be tolerated. No man will allow it in his field, and the only place for it is the street; and there it is cast to be trodden under foot of men."

Lamp. — Candles were not at this time used in Judea. The word in the common version is an incorrect rendering.

Prophets: I have not come to annul, but to complete. For truly I say to you, till heaven and earth pass away, not one jot or one tittle will pass away from the Law; not till all things are accomplished. Whoever, therefore, shall break one of the least of these commandments, and teach men so, will be the least in the kingdom of heaven; but whoever shall do and teach them, will be great in the kingdom of heaven. For I tell you, Unless your righteousness exceed that of the Scribes and Pharisees, you will by no means enter the kingdom of heaven.

You have heard that it was said to them of old, "Thou shalt do no murder, and whosoever commits murder shall be in danger of the Judges." But I say to you, whoever is angry with his brother, without cause, shall be in danger of the Judges; and whoever shall say to his brother, "Raca," shall be in danger of the Sanhedrim; but whoever shall say to his brother, "Thou fool," shall be in danger of the Gehenna of fire.

Therefore, if you bring your gift to the altar, and

The Judges.—Every city had its elders, who formed a court with power to determine minor matters. There were three of these elders, called judges, in the smaller cities, and twenty-three in the larger. The next higher body was the Sanhedrim, which acted on capital offences.

The Gehenna of Fire.—This refers to the Valley of Hinnom, a narrow ravine with steep and rocky sides,—near Jerusalem, on the south. In this valley the idolatrous Jews formerly conducted the worship to Moloch. Here infants were sacrificed, by being put into the arms of the idol—a brass image, heated by a great fire built within. No death could be more horrible, and no figure could more terribly express the torture enkindled in his own breast by the persistent and hardened violator of the laws of his being.

there remember that your brother has aught against you, leave your gift there before the altar, and go away; first be reconciled to your brother, and then come and offer your gift. Agree with your accuser quickly, while you are on the way with him, lest he bring you before the judge, and the judge deliver you to the officer, and you be cast into prison. Truly I tell you, you will not come out thence, till you have paid the last farthing.

You have heard that it was said: "Thou shalt not commit adultery." But I say to you, whoever looks on a woman to lust after her, has already committed adultery with her in his heart. And if your right eye lead you into sin, pluck it out and cast it from you; for it is better for you that one of your members should perish, than that your whole body should be cast into hell. And if your right hand lead you into sin, cut it off and cast it from you; for it is better for you that one of your members should perish, than that your whole body should be cast into hell.

It has been said: "Let him who would put away his wife give her a writing of divorcement." But I say to

A writing of Divorcement. — The Jews inferred from the Levitical law that a man might divorce his wife for any cause whatever. Their Rabbis said: "If a man sees a woman he loves better than his wife, let him divorce his wife, and marry her." The school of Hillel taught, that "If the wife cook her husband's food ill, by over salting or over roasting it, she is to be put away," also "If the wife by any stroke of God, become dumb, or foolish." Josephus relates of himself, that "about that time, I divorced my wife, who had borne me three children, not being pleased with her manners." Christianity alone has created domestic life, and made the union

you, whoever puts away his wife except for adultery, causes her to commit adultery; and whoever marries her who is put away, commits adultery.

Again, you have heard that it was said to them of old, "Thou shalt not forswear thyself, but shalt perform thine oaths to the Lord." But I say to you, Swear not at all; not by heaven, for it is God's throne; nor by the earth, for it is his footstool; neither by Jerusalem, for it is the city of the great King; neither swear by your head, for you cannot make one hair white or black. But let your manner of speech be Yea, yea; Nay, nay; for what is more than these, comes of evil.

You have heard that it was said, "An eye for an eye, and a tooth for a tooth." But I say to you, Resist not the evil-doer; but whoever shall smite you on the right cheek, turn to him the other also. And if any man would sue you at law to take away your coat, let him have your cloak also; and should one

of the sexes a sacred bond dissolvable only by death or crime.

Swear not at all. — All eastern nations are fearfully profane. Dr. Thomson says, speaking of the present people of Palestine, "everybody curses and swears when in a passion. No people that I have ever known can compare with the Orientals for profanity. The evil habit seems inveterate and universal. When Peter, therefore, began to curse and to swear on that dismal night of temptation, we are not to suppose that it was something foreign to his former habits."

Coat. — This was the tunic, a garment usually of linen, made to fit closely to the body, with short sleeves, and extending below the knees. Over it was worn the cloak, a square garment, wrapped loosely about the person, and laid aside when labor was performed. Of the former kind was

compel you to go one mile, go with him two. Give to him who asks of you, and from him who would borrow of you, turn not away.

You have heard that it was said, "Thou shalt love thy neighbor, and hate thine enemy:" But I say to you, Love your enemies, bless those who curse you, do good to those who hate you, and pray for those who despitefully use you and persecute you: that you may be children of your Father in heaven; for he makes his sun to rise on the evil and on the good, and sends his rain on the just and on the unjust.

For if you love those who love you, what praise do you deserve? Do not even the Gentiles the same? And if you salute your brethren only, what do you more than others? do not even the tax-gatherers so? And if you do good to those who do good to you, what praise do you deserve? sinners do even the same. And if you lend to those of whom you hope to receive, what praise do you deserve? sinners also lend to sinners, to receive as much in return. But do good, and lend, hoping for nothing in return; and your reward will be great, and you will be children of the Highest: for he is kind to the unthankful and to the evil. Be you, then, perfect, even as your Father in heaven is perfect.

the vesture without seam, woven throughout, for which lots were cast. (John xix. 23).

Should one compel you to go one mile. — It was a custom, introduced by the Persians and adopted by the Romans, to transmit intelligence by couriers, placed at regular distances. These couriers were authorized to impress horses or men for the public service, while on their journeys. The practice is still followed by the Turks, and resistance is punishable with death.

Take heed that you do not your good deeds to be seen by men; otherwise you have no reward of your Father in heaven. Therefore, when you give alms, do not sound a trumpet before you, as the hypocrites do, in the Synagogues, and in the streets, that men may give them honor. Truly, I say to you, they have their reward. But when you give alms, let not your left hand know what your right hand is doing; and your alms being in secret, your Father who sees in secret will reward you openly. And when you pray be not like the hypocrites, who are wont to pray standing in the Synagogues, and in the corners of the streets, to be seen by men. Truly, I say to you, they have their reward. But do you, when you pray, enter your closet, and having shut your door, pray to your Father who is in secret; and your Father who sees in secret, will reward you openly.

And when you pray, use not idle repetitions, as the heathen do; for they think they shall be heard for their many words. Be not you, then, like them; for

Who pray standing on the corners of the streets.—The Mahommedans of Palestine, when overtaken by the hour of prayer, suspend their employments and pray, even in the most public places. Spreading their outer garments on the ground, and turning their faces towards Mecca, they go through certain gestures, and forms of prayer, and then resume their previous employments, as if nothing had happened.

Idle repetitions.—The Jewish Rabbis taught that, "Whoever multiplies prayer is heard," "Whoever prolongs prayer, his prayer does not return to him empty, and he that is long in prayer, his days shall be prolonged." The Moslems are required to repeat some expressions thirty times, and others, as often as a hundred.

your Father knows what you need before you ask him. Do you, then, pray in this manner, Our Father who art in heaven, hallowed be thy name. Thy kingdom come. Thy will be done on earth, as it is in heaven. Give us this day our needful bread. Forgive us our debts, as we forgive our debtors. And bring us not into trial, but deliver us from evil.

For if you forgive men their offences, your heavenly Father will also forgive you: But if you forgive not men their offences, your Father will not forgive your offences.

Moreover, when you fast, be not like the hypocrites, of a sad countenance; for they disfigure their faces, that they may appear to men to fast. Truly, I say to you, They have their reward. But when you fast, anoint your head, and wash your face; that you may not appear to men to fast, but to your Father who is in secret; and your Father who sees in secret will reward you openly.

Lay not up for yourselves treasures on earth, where moths and worms consume, and where thieves break through and steal. But lay up for yourselves treasures in heaven, where neither moths nor worms consume, and where thieves do not break through nor steal. For where your treasure is, there your heart will be also.

The light of the body is the eye; therefore if your eye be clear your whole body will be full of light;

Anoint your head. — The richer class of Jews anointed their bodies daily with sweet or olive oil. The custom still exists among eastern nations. It preserves the skin soft, and in hot climates conduces greatly to health.

Worms. — An insect is here referred to which destroys wheat and other grains.

but if your eye be evil your whole body will be full of darkness. If, then, the light within you be dark, how great is your darkness!

No man can serve two masters; for he will hate one and love the other; or he will adhere to one, and neglect the other. You cannot serve God and Mammon.

For this reason I say to you; Be not anxious about your life, what you shall eat, or what you shall drink; nor yet for your body, what you shall put on. Is not life a greater gift than food, and the body than raiment? Behold the birds of the air, they neither sow nor reap, nor gather into barns; yet your heavenly Father feeds them. Are you not of more value than they? And who of you by being anxious can add one cubit to his stature?

And why are you anxious about raiment? Consider the lilies of the field, how they grow. They toil not, neither do they spin; and yet I tell you, that even Solomon in all his glory was not arrayed like one of these. And if God so clothes the grass of the field, which to-day is, and to-morrow is cast into the oven, will he not much more clothe you, O ye of little faith? Be not anxious, therefore, say-

Lilies. — A flower called the Hûleh lily grows luxuriantly among the hills of Nazareth, and on the borders of the Lake of Galilee. Dr. Thomson describes it as being very large, its three inner petals meeting above and forming a gorgeous canopy, such as art never approached, or King sat under. It is of a downy softness, the corolla white, but every petal marked with a single streak of bright purple down the middle. The gazelles feed upon it, and owing to the scarcity of fuel, it is, with the myrtle, rosemary, and cinnamon grasses, gathered and used in heating ovens.

ing, What shall we eat, or what shall we drink, or with what shall we be clothed? — all which things the Gentiles seek; — for your heavenly Father knows that you have need of them all; but seek you first the kingdom of God, and his righteousness, and all these things will be given you in addition. Therefore, be not anxious about the morrow; let the morrow care for itself. Enough for each day is its own evil.

Judge not, and you will not be judged; condemn not, and you will not be condemned; forgive, and you will be forgiven. Give, and it will be given to you; good measure, pressed down, shaken together, and running over, will men give into your bosom; for the same measure that you deal will be dealt to you again.

Why behold you the mote which is in your brother's eye, and perceive not the beam that is in your own eye? Or how can you say to your brother, Brother, let me pull out the mote that is in your eye, when you perceive not the beam that is in your own eye? Hypocrite! first cast the beam out of your own eye, and then you will see clearly to pull the mote out of your brother's eye.

Give not what is holy to dogs, nor cast your pearls before swine, lest the swine trample them under foot, and the dogs turn and rend you.

Ask, and it will be given you; seek, and you will find; knock, and the door will be opened to you. For every one that asks receives; and he that seeks, finds; and to him that knocks, the door will be opened. Who among you, if his son ask for bread, will give him a stone? Or if he ask for a fish, will give him a serpent? If you, then, though evil, give good gifts to your children, how much more will your Father in heaven give good gifts to those that ask him? Do, then, to others whatever you would that they should do to you; for this is the Law and the Prophets.

Enter you in at the strait gate; for wide is the gate, and broad is the way, that leads to destruction, and many go in thereat; because strait is the gate, and narrow the way, that leads to life, — and few there are that find it.

Beware of false teachers, who come to you in sheep's clothing, but inwardly are ravening wolves. You may know them by their fruits. Do men gather grapes of thorns, or figs of thistles? Every good tree brings forth good fruit; and every evil tree brings forth evil fruit. A good tree cannot bring forth evil fruit, nor can an evil tree bring forth good fruit. So, then, by their fruits you may know them. Every tree that brings not forth good fruit will be cut down, and cast into the fire.

Not every one who says to me, Lord, Lord, will

The Wide and Strait Gates. — Nearly every town in Syria and Palestine is surrounded with walls, and entered by gates. The principal ones are wide, two-leaved, plated with iron, closed with locks, and fastened with metal bars. The gateway is vaulted, shady, and cool, and so, is a favorite resort in the heat of the day. Dr. Thomson says, "I have seen the strait and narrow ways, 'with here and there a traveller.' They are in retired corners, and must be sought for. They are opened only to those who knock, and when the sun goes down, and the night comes on, are shut and locked."

enter the kingdom of heaven; but he who does the will of my Father who is in heaven. Many will say to me in that day, Lord, Lord, have we not taught to thy name? and in thy name cast out demons? and in thy name done many wonderful works? Yet shall I then declare to them, I never knew you; depart from me, ye who do iniquity.

Whoever, then, hears these words of mine and does them, I will liken to a wise man, who built a house, and dug deep, and set the foundation on a rock; and the rain descended, and the flood arose, and the winds blew, and beat vehemently on that house; and it fell not; for it was founded on a rock. And whoever hears these words of mine, and does them not, will be like a foolish man, who built his house upon the sand. And the rain descended, and the flood arose, and the winds blew, and beat upon that house; and it fell; and great was its fall.

And when Jesus had ended this discourse, the people were astonished at his teaching; for he taught as one having authority, and not as the teachers of the Law.*

And when he came down from the mountain, great multitudes followed him, and he entered Capernaum. And a certain centurion's servant, whom he held dear, was sick of the palsy, near to death. And hearing

Centurion.—The captain of a hundred men in the Roman army. He was generally from the better class of citizens, and often a man of fortune. Matthew describes the Centurion as coming to Jesus in person, and this he may have done after the elders had preferred their request.

* Matt. vi. viii. 1. Luke vi. 20-49.

of Jesus, he sent to him the elders of the Jews, to beg that he would come and cure his servant. And coming to Jesus, they besought him earnestly, saying, "He is worthy that you should do this for him; for he loves our nation, and it was he who built our synagogue." Jesus answered: "I will come and cure him," and he went with them. But when he was not far from the house, the centurion sent friends to him, to say, "Lord, trouble not yourself; for I am not worthy that you should come under my roof; nor do I myself think worthy to come to you; but only speak a word, and my servant will be cured. For even I, who am a man under command, have soldiers under me, and I say to one, Go, and he goes; and to another, Come, and he comes; and to my servant, Do this, and he does it." When Jesus heard this, he wondered at him, and turning round, he said to the people that followed, "Truly, I have not found such faith in Israel; and I tell you, that many will come from the east and the west, and will recline at table with Abraham, and Isaac, and Jacob, in the kingdom of heaven; but the children of the kingdom will be cast forth into the outer darkness, where will be weeping and gnashing of teeth." And Jesus said to those who were sent; "Go your way, as he has believed, so be it done to him." And returning they found the servant had been cured in the same hour.*

Many will come from the East and the West. — This declaration was addressed to Jews who considered it contamination to eat with Gentiles.

* Matt. viii. 5-13. Luke vii. 1-10.

And the day after, he went to a town called Nain; and numbers of his disciples and many people went with him. And when he was near the gate of the town, a dead man was borne out, the only son of his mother, and she was a widow; and many people of the town were with her. And when the Lord saw her he took pity on her, and said to her, "Weep not." And he went up and touched the bier; and the bearers stood still; and he said, "Young man, I say to thee, Rise." And the dead man sat up, and began to speak; and he gave him to his mother. Then all were struck with awe, and gave glory to God, saying, "A great prophet has risen up among us;" and, "God has visited his people."

And the report of this spread through all Judea, and all the region round about.* And the disciples

Nain — This town was about sixteen miles southwest from Capernaum, and near Mount Tabor, the brook Kishon, running between it and the foot of the mountain. It was once a place of considerable extent, but is now scarcely more than a cluster of ruins, tenanted only by a few Mohammedans. Its only antiquities are tombs, and a rock to the west of the village is full of them. The town is approached by a narrow road which rises abruptly from the plain of Esdraelon, and it was while coming up this way that Jesus met the widow and her son.

Borne Out. — All Jews, but those of the family of David, were buried outside the walls of towns. The bodies of persons above three years of age, were borne out on beds or biers, and long processions followed; the women leading the way and chanting a mournful dirge, and the rest lamenting and beating their breasts. So great respect was shown to the dead, that when one of even the common people was buried, all work was suspended.

Luke vii: 11-17.

of John told him, while he was in prison, of all these things, and he sent two of them to Jesus to ask, "Art thou he who was to come? or must we look for another?" And the men came to Jesus and said, "John, the Baptist, has sent us to you, to ask, Art thou he who was to come? or must we look for another?" Jesus immediately cured many of diseases and plagues, and of evil spirits; and gave sight to many who were blind, and then he answered, "Go, and tell John what you have seen and heard; how the blind see, the lame walk, the lepers are cleansed, the deaf hear, the dead are raised up, and the poor hear the glad tidings of the kingdom of heaven, — and that happy is he, who shall not be offended with me."

And when the messengers of John had departed, he said to the people concerning John, "What went you out to the desert to see? A reed shaken by the wind? Nay, then what went you out to see? A man clothed in fine raiment? Lo! those who wear fine raiment, and live in luxury are in kings' houses. But what went you out to see? A prophet? Yea, I say to you, and more than a prophet; for this is he, of whom it is written, 'Lo! I send my messenger before thy face, to prepare the way before thee.' Among those that are born of women a greater has not risen than John the Baptist; and yet the humblest in the kingdom of heaven is greater than he. And from the days of John the Baptist, until now, the kingdom of heaven suffers violence, and the violent take it by force. For all the prophets and the Law prophesied until the time of John; and, if you will receive it, he is the Elijah who was to come. He that has ears to hear, let him hear.

But to what shall I liken this generation? It is like children playing in the market-places, and calling to one another, 'We have piped to you, and you have not danced; we have wailed to you, and you have not lamented.' For John came neither eating bread nor drinking wine, and they say, 'He has a demon.' The Son of man has come eating and drinking, and they say, 'Lo! a gluttonous man and a wine-bibber, a friend of tax-gatherers and sinners.' Yet Wisdom is honored by her children." * And all the people that heard him, and the publicans, honored God and were baptized with the baptism of John. But the Pharisees and lawyers rejected the teachings of God, not being baptized of him.

Then he began to reprove the towns in which most of his mighty works had been done, because they had not repented. "Alas for thee, Chorazin! Alas for thee, Bethsaida! for if the mighty works had been done in Tyre and Sidon which have been done in you, they

Market Places, were areas, generally near the gates of the cities, one side of which was occupied by the market, the others by the courts of justice and other public buildings. In these open places the doctors met, and conversed, and people gathered for business or amusement, and here children also collected and practised their games, in which, of course, they imitated the graver customs of their elders. Instrumental music, — or piping — and dancing, was practised at marriages, and wailing at funerals.

Chorazin and Bethsaida. — These towns were not far from Capernaum, but their precise location is not known. They were destroyed in the wars between the Jews and Romans.

Tyre and Sidon, were rich trading cities noted for their

*Matt. xi. 2-19. Luke vii. 18-35.

would have repented long ago in sackcloth and ashes. And I say to you, It will be more tolerable for Tyre and Sidon in the day of Judgment, than for you. And thou Capernaum! that hast been exalted to heaven, thou wilt be brought down to hell; for if the mighty works had been done in Sodom, which have been done in thee, it would have remained until this day. And I say to you, it will be more tolerable for Sodom, in the day of Judgment, than for you."

At that time Jesus said, "I thank thee, O Father, Lord of heaven and earth, because thou hast hid these things from the wise and discerning, and hast revealed them to babes. Yea, Father, for so it has seemed good in thy sight. All things are given to me by my Father; and no one knows the Son, but the Father; neither knows any one the Father, but the Son, and he to whom the Son will reveal him."

"Come unto me all ye that labor, and are heavy laden, and I will give you rest. Take my yoke upon you, and learn of me; for I am meek and lowly in heart; and you will find rest for your souls. For my yoke is easy, and my burden is light." *

And one of the Pharisees asked him to eat with

pride, luxury, and contempt of religion. Judges xviii. 7. Isaiah xxiii. 9. Amos i. 9, 10.

And one of the Pharisees asked him to eat with him.—The Jews had only two meals, a light one—the breakfast—at about eleven or twelve o'clock in the day, and a more bountiful one—the dinner—at sunset. The table was but slightly elevated from the ground, and the guests reclined about it on low couches, which were placed around three of its sides, an opening being left at the fourth for the entrance of the ser-

*Matt. xi. 20-30.

him, and going into the Pharisees house, he reclined at his table. And a woman of the city, who was a sinner, hearing that Jesus was at table in the Pharisees house, brought an alabaster box of ointment, and standing behind him at his feet, weeping, began to wet his feet with tears, and to wipe them with the hair of her head; and she kissed his feet, and anointed them with the ointment. But when the Pharisee who

vants who served at the meal. Ordinarily only three persons, but sometimes four or five, reclined on each couch. The couches were provided with cushions, on which the guest rested upon his left elbow, his right arm being free, and his feet extended outward from the table, so that one standing at them would be behind him. When several guests reclined on one couch their bodies overlapped, and the one next below another, rested his head on or near the breast of the one behind him. Next to the host was the place of honor, and the guest occupying it was said to "lie in his bosom," (John i. 18, xiii. 23, xxi. 20). Knives and forks were not used, and each person took his food with his hand from a common dish. A piece of bread was held between the thumb and two fore fingers, and was dipped either into a bowl of melted grease, (this was the "sop" John xiii. 26,) or into a dish of meat, whence a piece was conveyed to the mouth between two layers of bread. When guests were invited more than ordinary ceremony was used, and it was to the neglect of this ceremony on the part of Simon, that Jesus alluded. On such occasions the visitor was received with a kiss, water was produced to wash his feet, and his head, and often his beard and feet, were perfumed with oil.

Kissed his feet.—Among ancient nations kissing the feet was a token of deep reverence, and earnest supplication. Seneca relates that "C. Cæsar gave wine to Pompey Pennus, whom he had pardoned, and then, on his returning thanks, presented his left foot for him to kiss." Xenophon speaks of similar instances. From this arose the custom of kissing the Pope's foot.

had invited him, saw this, he said to himself, "This man, if he were a prophet, would know who and what this woman is who is touching him, for she is a sinner." And Jesus said to him, "Simon, I have something to say to you;" and he said, "Teacher, say on." And Jesus said, "A certain creditor had two debtors: the one owed him five hundred denarii, the other fifty, and both having nothing to pay, he freely forgave them both. Tell me, therefore, which of them will love him most?" Simon answered, "I suppose he to whom he forgave most." And Jesus said to him, "You have judged rightly." Then, turning to the woman, he said to Simon, "See you this woman? I entered your house, you gave me no water for my feet; but she has wet them with tears, and wiped them with the hairs of her head. You gave me no kiss; but since I came in, she has not ceased to kiss my feet. My head with oil you did not anoint; but she has anointed my feet with ointment. Therefore, I say to you, her sins, which are many, are forgiven; for she has loved much, but he to whom little

Denarii. — Roman silver coin then in circulation in Palestine. One denarius, it would seem from Matt. xx. 1-13, was then the ordinary pay for a day's labor. Fifty were equal to about seven dollars, five hundred to seventy.

No water for my feet. — As sandals were worn which covered only the sole of the foot, frequent washings were necessary. It was customary to remove the sandals and bathe the feet whenever one entered a house, and in omitting to provide water for this purpose, Simon had neglected one of the commonest acts of hospitality. In Hindoostan, at the present time, when a superior enters the house of an inferior, the latter brings water, and washes his feet.

is forgiven, he loves little." Then he said to the woman, "Your sins are forgiven." And those that were at table with him said to themselves, "Who is this that even forgives sins." But he said to the woman, "Your faith has saved you; go in peace." *

And afterward he went through all the towns and villages preaching the glad tidings of the kingdom of God; and the twelve went with him, also certain women, whom he had cured of evil spirits and infirmities,—Mary, called Mary of Magadala, out of whom had gone seven demons, and Joanna, the wife of Chuza, Herod's steward, and Susanna, and many others, who provided for him from their property.†

And as they went into a certain house, the multitude came together so that they could not so much as eat bread. And when his kinsmen heard of this they went out to lay hold of him, for they said "He is beside himself."

Then a blind and dumb man possessed by a demon, was brought to him; and he healed him, so that the blind, and dumb both spake and saw.

Mary of Magdala.—Magdala was on the sea of Galilee, south of Capernaum. Mary is commonly supposed to have been an abandoned character, but of this there is no evidence. From this notice it is to be inferred that she was a person of some property.

Seven Demons.—The Jews supposed the demons who possessed men were the spirits of mortals who, after death, haunted the earth, and under the direction of Satan, worked evil to mankind. In aggravated cases seven were thought to tenant the body of one person.

*Luke vii. 30-49.
†Luke viii. 1-3.

When the demon had gone out, all the people wondered, and said, "Is not this the Son of David?" But when the Pharisees, who had come down from Jerusalem, heard of it, they said, "He casts out demons, but only by Beelzebub, the prince of demons." And Jesus, knowing their thoughts, called them to him, and said, "Every kingdom at war within itself is laid waste; and every city or family at discord within itself is brought to ruin. If Satan cast out Satan he is at war with himself; how then can his kingdom stand? And if I by Beelzebub cast out demons, by whom do your disciples cast them out? Therefore they shall be your judges; but if I, by the spirit of God, cast out demons then has the kingdom of God come among you. How can one enter a strong man's house and seize upon his goods, without first binding the strong man? Then may he plunder his house. He that is not with me is against me, and he that gathers not with me, scatters abroad; and truly, I say to you, all manner of sin and calumny may be forgiven to men; but the calumny against the spirit of God may not be forgiven. Whoever speaks against the Son of Man may be forgiven; but whoever speaks against the spirit of God will not be forgiven, neither in this world, nor in the world to come." (This, he said, because they accused him of having an evil spirit).

"Admit that the tree is good, and its fruit good, or else that the tree is bad, and its fruit bad; for a tree is known by its fruit. O brood of vipers! how can you

By whom do your Disciples cast them out? — For proof that the Jews practised exorcism see Acts xix. 13. Mark ix. 38. Luke ix. 49. Josephus, Antiq, lib. viii.

who are evil, speak what is good, for out of the abundance of the heart the mouth speaks. A good man out of the good treasure of his heart brings forth what is good, and an evil man, out of the evil treasure, brings forth what is evil. And I say to you, that for every vile word that men speak they will give account in a day of Judgment; for according to your words you will be justified, and according to your words you will be condemned." *

And while the people were thronging thickly about him, certain of the Scribes and Pharisees, to make trial of him, said, "Teacher, show us a sign from heaven." But he answered them, "This is an evil generation. It seeks a sign; but no sign shall be given it, but the sign of the prophet Jonah; for as Jonah was three days and three nights in the heart of the fish, and a sign to the Ninevites; so shall the Son of Man be three days and three nights in the heart of the earth, and a sign to this generation. The men of Nineveh will rise before the Judgment seat with this generation, and will condemn it; for they repented, at the preaching of Jonah, and lo! a greater than Jonah is here. The queen of the south will rise before the Judgment seat with this generation, and

A sign from heaven. — Some supernatural appearance in the air. They ascribed what he had done to the power of Satan; but this, they implied, would convince them. Some such sign they appear to have expected from the coming Messiah.

Rise before the Judgment seat. — An allusion to the custom among the Jews and Romans for witnesses to rise from their seats, when accusing, or giving evidence against, criminals.

*Mark iii. 19-30. Matt. xii. 22-37. Luke xi. 14, 15, 17, 23.

will condemn it; for she came from the ends of the earth to hear the wisdom of Solomon, and lo! a greater than Solomon is here. When a foul spirit has gone out of a man he walks through desert places, seeking rest and finding none. Then he says, I will return to my house whence I came; and returning, he finds it empty, swept, and set in order. Then he goes and takes with him seven other spirits more wicked than himself, and they enter in, and dwell there; and the last state of the man, is worse than the first. So will it be with this wicked generation.*

While he was speaking, a certain woman called out from the throng, "Blessed is the womb that bore thee, and the breasts that thou hast nursed." But he said, "Rather, blessed are those who hear the word of God, and keep it." While he thus talked to the people his mother and his kinsmen came and stood without, desiring to speak with him. But not being able to get to

Through desert places. — The common notion was that evil spirits haunted dry and desert places.

That man. — Reference is here made to the whole nation of Jews. Jesus compares them to a demoniac, who, after an interval of quiet, relapses into greater violence. Since their return from Babylon, the Jews had not fallen into idolatry, and, therefore, did not consider themselves liable to the anger of God; but Jesus says that seven demons are about to enter them, and their last state will be worse than the first. According to Josephus, "the character of the Jews, just before their final destruction by the Romans, was the vilest that can be conceived. They pressed on to their own ruin as if they were possessed by legions of devils, and wrought up to the last degree of madness."

*Matt. xii. 38-45. Luke xi. 24-36.

him on account of the multitude, they sent to him, calling him, and those who sat about him said, "Lo! Your mother and your kinsmen are without, asking for you." And he answered, "Who is my mother, or my kinsmen?" and looking round on those about him, he stretched forth his hand towards his disciples, and said, "Behold my mother and my kinsmen; for whoever does the will of my Father in heaven is my brother, and my sister, and my mother." *

And when he had finished speaking, a certain Pharisee asked him to dine with him, and he went into his house and reclined at his table. But the Pharisee wondered when he saw that he did not wash before dinner. And the Lord said to him, "Now, you Pharisees make clean the outside of your cups and dishes, but your inward part is full of rapacity and wickedness. Fools! did not He who made the outside, make the inside also? But give alms of what you have, and all things will be clean to you. Alas, for you Pharisees! for you give tithes of mint and rue, and all manner of herbs, and pass by justice, and the love of God. These ought you to have done, and not to have left the other undone. Alas, for you Pharisees! for you love the highest seats in the synagogues, and greetings in the market-places. Alas, for you, Scribes and Pharisees! Hypocrites! you are like

Rue. — A small shrub grown in gardens. It has a strong smell, and a bitter taste, and is used in medicine. Paying tithes on these insignificant herbs shows how scrupulous the Pharisees were in observing all the minor requirements of their religion.

*Matt. xii. 38–45. Mark iii. 31–35.

hidden graves which men walk over, and are not aware of."

Then one of the teachers of the Law said to him, "Teacher, in saying this, you reproach us also." And he answered, "Alas for you, lawyers, also! for you load men with burdens grievous to be borne, and you, yourselves, touch them not with one of your fingers. Alas for you, for you build the sepulchres of the prophets, and your fathers killed them. Truly you show that you approve of the deeds of your fathers; for they slew them, and you build their sepulchres. Alas for you, lawyers! for you have taken away the key of knowledge; you enter not yourselves, and you keep out those who are entering."

Hidden Graves. — The graves of the common people were mere excavations in the earth, sodded, and level with the ground.

Build their Sepulchres. — The Jews greatly reverenced the tombs of dead men. Dr. Thomson says that in Palestine at the present time, "every village has its saints' tombs — every hill-top is covered with the white dome of some prophet. Thither all resort to garnish the sepulchres, burn incense and consecrated candles, fulfil vows, make offerings and pray. So fanatical are they in their zeal that they would tear any one to pieces, who should put dishonor on one of the sacred shrines. Enter that at Hebron, for example, and they would instantly sacrifice you to their fury. It was for rebuking this, and other kinds of idolatry, that 'their fathers killed the prophets,' and those who built their tombs would, in like manner, kill any one who denounced *their* idolatrous reverence for these very sepulchres." Thus the Pharisees were actuated by the same spirit as their fathers.

The Key of Knowledge. — When the Scribe was admitted to his office, the presiding Rabbi solemnly delivered to him the "key of knowledge," with which he was to open and shut

When he had said these things to them, the Scribes and Pharisees began to press him vehemently with questions about many things, hoping to ensnare him into some words that might serve for an accusation against him.

In the mean time thousands of the people had gathered together, so that they trod one upon another, and he began to say to his disciples. "First of all, beware you of the leaven of the Pharisees, which is hypocrisy; for nothing is covered that will not be revealed, nor hidden that will not be made known. Therefore, whatever you have spoken in darkness, will be heard in the light, and what you have whispered in closets, will be proclaimed from the house-tops; and I say to you, my friends, fear not those who kill the body, and after that can do no more, but I will warn you whom to fear; Fear Him, who after he has killed, has power to cast into hell. Yea I say to you, fear Him. Are not five sparrows sold for two farth-

the treasures of Divine wisdom; and he is said to have worn the figure of a key on his garment, as a symbol of his office.

Proclaimed from the house tops. — The roofs of Jewish houses were flat, and were greatly resorted to by all classes of people. Dr. Thomson states that "at the present day the governors in country districts [of Palestine], cause their commands to be published from the house-tops. Their proclamations are generally made in the evening, after the people have returned from their labors in the field. The public crier ascends the highest roof at hand, and lifts up his voice in a long-drawn call upon all faithful subjects to give ear and obey.

Fear not those who kill the body. —Jesus had just endangered his own life by his severe denunciation of the Pharisees.

Sparrows. — The sparrows of Judea are described as tame,

ings, and yet not one of them is forgotten before God. Nay, even the very hairs of your head are all numbered. Fear not, therefore, you are of more value than many sparrows. Also, I say to you, whoever shall acknowledge me before men, him will the Son of Man also acknowledge before the angels of God."

And one among the multitude said to him, "Teacher, speak to my brother that he divide the inheritance with me;" but Jesus said to him, "Man, who made me a judge, or a divider over you?" And he said to his disciples, "Take heed, and beware of covetousness; for a man's life consists not in the abundance of his possessions." And he spoke a parable to them, saying, "The ground of a certain rich man yielded abundantly, and he thought to himself, What shall I do, for I have no room to store my grain. Then he said, This will I do. I will pull down my barns, and build greater, and in them, I will store all my fruits and produce. And I will say to my soul, Soul, thou hast many good things laid up for many years, take thine ease, eat, drink, and be merry. But God said to him, Thou fool! this night thy soul will be required of thee. Then whose will all this be that thou hast provided? So is he who lays up treasure for himself, and is not rich toward God.

troublesome and impertinent birds infesting the towns, in countless numbers. They are not much valued for food, and are snared and destroyed as a public nuisance.

Divide the inheritance. — Among the Jews the older brother had two shares, the rest was divided equally among the remaining children. The word Judge here means arbitrator, and the doctors of the law acted in that capacity in family disputes.

"Fear not, little flock, for it has pleased your Father to give you the kingdom. Sell what you have, and give to the poor, provide yourselves purses that wax not old, a treasure in the heavens, that will not fail, where no thief will come, and no moth destroy, for where your treasure is, there will your heart be also. Let your loins be girt about, and your lamps burning, and be you like men who wait their lord's return from the wedding, that when he comes and knocks, they may open to him immediately. Happy will be those servants, whom the Lord when he comes shall find watching. Truly, I say to you, he will gird himself, and place them at table, and come forth and serve them. And whether he come in the second watch, or come in the third, happy will be those servants who are thus found watching. And this you know, that if the master of a house knows at what hour the thief is coming, he is awake, and suffers not his house to be broken into. Be you then always ready; for in an hour when you think not the Son of Man will come."

Then Peter said to him, "Lord, speak you this parable to us, or even to all?" And the Lord said,

Let your loins be girt about. — The outer garment, when one walked or labored, was girded up about the waist with a sash or girdle.

Return from the Wedding. — Marriages were performed at night at the house of the bride's father, and the husband took his wife directly to his own house, where the wedding feast was given.

The second watch. — The night was divided by the Jews and Romans into four watches. The first was from six o'clock till nine P. M., the second from nine till twelve, the third from twelve till three A. M., and the fourth from three till six.

"'Who then is the faithful, and wise steward whom his lord will make ruler over his household, to give them their food in due season?' He is that servant whom his lord when he comes shall find so doing. Happy is he! for of a truth I say to you, his lord will make him ruler over all that he has. But should the servant say in his heart, My lord delays his coming, and should begin to beat the men-servants, and the maidens, and to eat and drink and be drunken, the lord of that servant will come in a day when he looks not for him, and in an hour when he is not aware, and will cut him asunder, and assign him his portion with the unfaithful. And that servant who knows his lord's will, and prepares not himself, nor does according to his will, will be beaten with many stripes; but he who knows it not, though he does things worthy of stripes, will be beaten with few; for to whom much is given, of him much will be required; and to whom even men commit much, of him they ask the more.

"I came to send fire on the earth, and what would I if it were already kindled. But I have a baptism, to

Cut him asunder. — Cutting asunder was a mode of capital punishment practised by the Persians and Chaldeans. The left hand and right foot, or the right hand and left foot, or both hands and both feet, were taken off at the joints, and the criminal was allowed to bleed to death. It was practised also among the Jews, as is seen from 2 Samuel xii. 31. 1 Samuel xv. 33. 1 Kings iii. 25. Hebrews xi. 37, and the Hebrew tradition is that Isaiah was "sawn asunder in the midst" whilst alive. It is still practised among the Moors of Barbary.

Few Stripes. — The Jews inflicted not more than forty stripes for any one offence. Deut. xxv. 3: and servants were not generally treated with severity.

be baptized with, and how am I straightened till it be accomplished! Suppose you that I have come to bring peace on the earth? I tell you nay, but only division. Henceforth, five in one house will be divided, three against two, and two against three, the father against the son, and the son against the father, the mother against the daughter, the daughter against the mother, the mother-in-law against the daughter-in-law, and the daughter-in-law against the mother-in-law, and a man's foes will be those of his own household." And he said also to the multitude, "When you see a cloud rising in the west, you say, There comes a shower; and so it is: and when the south-wind blows, you say, There will be heat; and so it is. You hypocrites! you can judge of the face of the sky, and of the earth, but how is it that you do not discern this time? Yea, and why even of yourselves judge you not what is right.* "

At that time, there were present, some who told him of the Galileans, whose blood Pilate had mingled with

A cloud in the West.— Rain-storms in Palestine come from the west — the Mediterranean; and the hot winds from the sultry deserts at the South.

The Galileans. — This incident is not mentioned by Josephus; but he says that the Galileans were distinguished above the other Jews for their seditions and turbulent disposition. He mentions several tumults which occurred at festivals, one — about thirty years before this — when Arcelaus massacred a large number of Jews, principally Galileans, in the temple at the feast of the Passover. A similar massacre occurred under Sabinus, the Roman Procurator, at the Feast of Pentecost.

* Luke xii. 1-59.

their sacrifices, and Jesus said to them, "Suppose you that those Galileans, because they suffered thus, were sinners above all the Galileans? I tell you, nay, but unless you repent, you will all in like manner perish. Or those eighteen on whom the tower in Siloam fell, and slew them; think you that they were greater sinners than all the dwellers in Jerusalem? I tell you, nay, but unless you repent, you will all in like manner perish." He spake also this parable. "A certain man had a fig-tree planted in his vineyard, and he came, seeking fruit on it, and found none. Then said he to the vine dresser, 'Lo! these three years have I come, seeking fruit from this fig-tree, and have found none. Cut it down! Why cumbers it the ground?' But the vine dresser answered, 'Lord, leave it for this year longer, that I may dig about it, and cast in manure; perhaps it may bear fruit; if not, then cut it down.'" *

The same day Jesus went out from the house, and taught by the seaside, and a great multitude came to him, so that he entered a boat and sat in the sea, while all the people stood by the sea on the land. And he taught them many things in parables, and in his teaching, said, "Hearken! A sower went forth to sow; and as he sowed, some seed fell by the

The Fig-tree, — is exhaustive of the soil, and very difficult of cultivation. To make it produce well it is necessary to plow and dig about it frequently, and to manure the roots thoroughly.

A sower went forth to sow. — "There is a nice and close adherence to actual life in this form of expression. It implies that the sower in the days of our Saviour lived in a hamlet or village as all these [Palestine] farmers now do;

* Luke xiii. 1–9.

way side, and was trodden down, and the birds came and devoured it. And some fell on stony ground, where was not much earth, and it sprang up quickly, because it had no depth of earth; but when the sun came up it was scorched, and, because it had no root, it withered away. And some fell among thorns, and the thorns grew up and choked it, so that it yielded no fruit. But other fell on good ground, and sprang up, yielding fruit, some thirty, some sixty, and some a hundred fold. He that has ears to hear, let him hear."

And when he was alone his disciples said to him, "Why speak you to the people in parables?" "Be-

that he did not sow near his own house, or in a garden fenced or walled, for such a field does not furnish all the basis of the parable. There are neither roads, nor thorns, nor stony places in such lots. He must *go forth* into the open country as those have done, where there are no fences, where the path passes through the cultivated land; where thorns grow in clumps all around; where the rocks peep out in places through the scanty soil; and where, also, hard by, are patches extremely fertile. Now, here we have the farm within a dozen rods of us. Our horses are actually trampling down some seeds which have fallen by the wayside, and larks and sparrows are busy picking them up. That man, with his mattock, is digging about places where the rock is too near the surface for the plough, and much that is sown there will wither away, because it has no deepness of earth. And not a few seeds have fallen among this *billan*, and will be effectually choked by this most tangled of thorn-bushes. But a large portion, after all, falls into really good ground, and four months hence will exhibit every variety of crop, up to the richest and hardiest that ever rejoices the heart of even an American farmer." — DR. W. M. THOMSON, in the *Land and the Book*.

cause," he answered, "it is given to you to know the new truths of the kingdom of heaven, but to them it is not given. For whoever has, to him more is given, and he has abundance; but whoever has not, from him is taken even what he seems to have. Hence, I speak to them in parables, because seeing they do not see, and hearing they do not hear, nor do they understand. And in them is fulfilled the prophecy of Isaiah which says, 'They will hear indeed, but will not understand, and see indeed, but not perceive; for this people's heart is waxed gross, and their ears are dull of hearing, and their eyes they have closed, lest they should see with their eyes, and hear with their ears, and understand with their hearts, and turn from their ways, and I should heal them.' But blessed are your eyes, for they see, and your ears, for they hear; for I say to you that many prophets and righteous men have desired to see what you see, and have not seen; and to hear what you hear, and have not heard. Hear, then, the parable of the sower: The seed is the word of God. When any one hears and understands it not, the Evil One comes and catches away what was sown in his heart. He is the seed sown by the way side. And the seed sown on stony ground is he who hears the word, and at once with joy receives it. But having no root in himself, he endures for but a time, and when tribulation or persecution comes on account of the word, he falls away. The seed among the thorns, is he who hears the word, and the cares of this

Waxed Gross. — The ancients had the idea that the fat of the body is destitute of sensation. Hence a "fat heart" denoted stupidity and lack of feeling.

world, and the deceitfulness of riches choke it, so that he becomes unfruitful. But the seed that fell on good ground, are they who hear the word and understand it, and also bear fruit, some thirty, some sixty, and some a hundred fold. If any man has ears to hear, let him hear." *

Another parable put he forth to the people, saying, "The kingdom of heaven is like a man who sowed good seed in his field, but the enemy came while his men slept, and sowed tares among the wheat, and went away. Now, when the blade came up and bore fruit, the tares appeared also. So the servants of the householder came and said to him, 'Sir, did you not sow good seed in your field? Whence, then, has it tares?' He said to them, 'An enemy has done this.' Then his servants said to him, 'Shall we go

While men slept. — Owing to the extreme heat, laborers in the East do no work in the middle of the day. Then they sleep.

Tares grow in great profusion all over the East, and are a great nuisance to the farmer. They closely resemble wheat, and until the stalk begins to head out, cannot be distinguished from the good grain. Though the farmers weed their fields, they do not attempt to separate the tares from the wheat; the two are so much alike, and their roots are so intertwined, that there is danger of pulling up both. They are therefore allowed to grow together until the harvest, when the stalks are mostly separated by hand, but if any remain among the wheat, the grain being lighter and smaller than that of the wheat, is easily separated by the winnowing fan. The grain of tares has a bitter taste, and, eaten separately or diffused among the wheat, produces dizziness and vomiting. The Arabic name is *Zowan.*

* Matt. xiii. 1–23. Mark iv. 1–25. Luke xiii. 4–18.

and weed them out?' But he said, 'No; lest while you weed out the tares, you root up the wheat along with them. Let both grow together until the harvest, and when the harvest comes I will say to the reapers, Collect together first the tares, and bind them in bundles to burn them; but gather the wheat into my barn.'"

Another parable put he forth to them, saying, "The kingdom of heaven is like a grain of mustard seed, that a man sowed in his field; which, though one of the least of all seeds, is, when grown, the greatest among herbs, and becomes a tree, so that the birds of the air rest on its branches."

And still another parable spake he to them. "The kingdom of heaven is like leaven, which a woman mixed in three measures of meal, till the whole was leavened."

All these things Jesus spake in parables, and without a parable he did not speak to them. But when they were alone he explained them all to his disciples. And thus were fulfilled the words of the prophet, "I will open my mouth in parables. I will utter

A grain of mustard seed.—The mustard plant grows wild, and in great luxuriance, near the Sea of Galilee. It bears a yellow flower, and grows to an enormous size, shooting forth great branches, so that the birds of the air come and lodge in its branches. It is sometimes seen as high as a horse and his rider. It is said to have been cultivated in earlier times, and to have then grown to such a size that a man could climb into it.

Three measures of meal.—Perhaps the ephah (Ex. xvi. 36. Ruth ii. 17), a measure of about a peck and a half, and probably the quantity usually taken in making bread. Genesis xvii. 6. 1 Samuel i. 24.

things which have been hidden from the foundation of the world."

Then Jesus, sending the multitude away, went into the house, and his disciples came to him, saying, "Explain to us the parable of the tares in the field." He answered them, "He who sows the good seed is the Son of Man. The seed is the word. The good seed are the children of the kingdom; but the tares are the children of the Evil One. The enemy who sowed them is the Devil, the harvest is the end of the age, and the reapers are angels. As, then, the tares are gathered and burned in the fire, so will it be at the end of the age. The Son of Man will send forth his angels, and they will gather from his kingdom all that lead to sin, and do iniquity, and will cast them into a furnace of fire, where will be wailing and gnashing of teeth. Then will the righteous shine as the sun in the kingdom of their Father. Who has ears to hear, let him hear."

"Again the kingdom of heaven is like treasure hidden in a field, which a man having found, keeps secret, and rejoicing, goes and sells all that he has, and buys that field."

The end of the age. — The word here rendered "age" was used by the Jews to denote the end of the state of things which was to precede the coming of the Messiah, and not the end of the world. Every reader will put his own interpretation on the meaning which Jesus intended to convey.

Furnace of Fire. — This figure is evidently drawn from the custom of burning alive, mentioned in Daniel iii. 10.

Treasure hidden in a Field. — Judea had been subject to invasions and calamities, and hence a feeling of insecurity had arisen among the people, and it had become a custom to hide treasures in fields and gardens. The practice is alluded

"Again, the kingdom of heaven is like a merchant seeking pearls, who, having found one of great price, goes and sells all that he has, and buys it."

"Again, the kingdom of heaven is like a net cast into the sea, which gathers of every kind; and being full, they draw to shore, and sitting down, gather the good into baskets, but cast the bad away. So will it be when the angels come forth and separate the wicked from the good, and cast them into the furnace of fire, where will be wailing and gnashing of teeth." And he also said, "The kingdom of heaven is as if a man should cast seed into the ground, and while he sleeps, and rises night and day, the seed should spring up and grow, he knows not how; for the earth brings forth of itself, first the blade, then the ear, after that the ripe grain in the ear. But when the grain is ripe, immediately he puts in the sickle, because the time of harvest has come." *

Jesus said to them, "Have you understood all these things?" They said to him, "Yes, Teacher." Then

to by Solomon (Prov. ii. 4). It still continues in Palestine, and the country is said to abound in hidden treasure. The right of treasure-trove was adjudged by Jewish law to the buyer, and not to the seller of the field.

A net cast into the Sea. — The great drag net is here referred to. In working it "some must row the boat, some cast out the net, some, on the shore, pull the rope with all their strength, others throw stones and beat the water round the ends, to frighten the fish from escaping, and, as it approaches the shore, all must be active in holding up the edges, drawing it to the land, and seizing the fish. Then the fishermen sit down, gather the good into baskets, and cast the bad away."

* Mark iv. 26–34.

he said to them, "Every one instructed in the kingdom of heaven, is like the master of a household who brings out of his storehouse things new and old." *

And when Jesus had finished these parables he departed thence.

And the same day in the evening, seeing great multitudes about him, he said to his disciples, "Let us go over to the other side of the lake." And as they were in the way, a certain Scribe came and said to him, "Lord, I will follow you wherever you go." And Jesus said to him, "Foxes have holes, and birds of the air have nests, but the Son of Man has not where to lay his head." And he said to another, "Follow me;" but the man answered, "Let me first go and bury my father." Jesus said to him, "Let the dead bury their dead, but go you and preach the kingdom of God." And another also said, "Lord I will follow you, but let me first go and bid farewell to my family." Jesus answered, "No man having put his hand to the plough, and looking back, is fit for the kingdom of God."

And when they had sent away the multitude, the disciples took him with them, as he was in the boat, to cross over to the other side. And there came down a great storm on the lake, and the waves dashed

A great storm came down on the Lake. — "To understand," says Dr. Thomson, "the causes of these violent tempests, we must remember that the lake lies low, — six hundred feet lower than the ocean, — that the vast and naked plateaus of Jaulan rise to a great height, spreading backward to the wilds of Hauran, and upward to snowy Hermon; that the water-courses have cut out profound ravines and wild gorges,

* Matt. xiii. 24–52.

over the boat, so that they were in jeopardy. Jesus was in the after part of the boat, asleep on a cushion, and they awoke him, saying, "Lord save us, we perish." Then he arose, and rebuked the wind, and said to the sea, "Peace, be still." And the wind ceased, and there was a great calm. He said to them, "Why are you so fearful? How is it that you have no faith?" And they feared exceedingly, and said to one another, "What manner of man is this, that even the wind and the sea obey him."

And when they had arrived at the other side of the lake, in the country of the Gerasenes, which is over

converging to the head of this lake, and that these act like gigantic funnels to draw down the winds from the mountains." Mr. N. C. Prime, who was cast away in a small boat in a sudden storm on this lake, describes the scene as follows: "We ran three or four miles up the west coast in good style, and then there came down on the sea such a storm as it knew in times of old. It was sudden, swift, and violent. A moment before, we were sailing along pleasantly over the rippling water, and now it was lashed into foam by a fierce blast that literally *came down* into the basin, and ploughed up the waters into deep and difficult furrows. I did not believe it possible that the little lake could get up such a sea as now rolled and tossed us." It will be noticed that Luke also says that "the storm *came down* on the lake." This is one of those instances of truthful local coloring in which the gospel narratives abound.

The Country of the Gerasines. — In speaking of the locality of this miracle, Dr. Thomson remarks: "In this Gersa, or Chersa, we have a position which fulfils every requirement of the narratives, and with a name so near that in Matthew as to be, in itself, a strong corroboration of the truth of this identification. It is within a few rods of the shore, and an immense mountain rises directly above it, in which are ancient

against Galilee, there met him, as he landed from the boat, two men possessed with demons, coming out of

tombs, out of some of which the two men, possessed of the devils, may have issued to meet Jesus. The lake is so near the base of the mountain that the swine, rushing madly down it, could not stop, but would be hurried on into the water and drowned. The place is one which our Lord would be likely to visit, having Capernaum in full view to the north, and Galilee "over against it," as Luke says it was (Luke viii. 26). The *name*, moreover, pronounced by Bedâwin Arabs is so similar to Gergasa, that to all my inquiries for this place they invaribly said it was at Chersa, and they insisted that they were identical, and I agree with them in their opinion. Everywhere [else], along the north-eastern and eastern shores, a smooth beach declines gently down to the water. But take your stand a little south of this Chersa. A great herd of swine, we will suppose, is feeding on this mountain that towers above it. They are seized with a sudden panic, rush madly down the almost perpendicular declivity, those behind tumbling over and thrusting forward those before, and, as there is neither time nor space to recover on the narrow shelf between the base and the lake, they are crowded headlong into the water, and perish. All is perfectly natural just at this point, and here, I suppose it did occur. Farther south the plain becomes so broad that the herd might have recovered and recoiled from the lake, whose domains they would not willingly invade." Gersa was a small place and unknown, while Gadara, — located some sixteen miles distant, — was a large Greek city celebrated for its temples, theatres, and warm baths. Therefore Mark and Luke, writing for Greeks, spoke of the country of the Gadarenes, while Matthew, writing for the Jews, spoke of that of the Gergasenes. One district included the other, and hence there is no contradiction in the accounts, but a natural adaptation to those for whom they were written.

Two men possessed with Demons. — Matthew mentions two, while Mark and Luke speak of only one. It was a maxim

the tombs where they had their dwelling. They were

of LeClerc that, "He who speaks of two, includes also the one; he who mentions only one, does not deny the two." Matthew is general in his description; Mark and Luke more detailed and graphic; and these peculiarities run through their entire narratives. The Jews attributed nearly all nervous disorders to demonical possession, and the Mohammedans of the present day hold the same opinion. Dr. Thomson, in his very valuable work, "THE LAND AND THE BOOK," referring to this subject, says: "In Sidon there are cases of epileptic fits which, in external manifestations, closely resemble that mentioned in Mark ix. 18, Matthew xvii. 15, and Luke ix. 38. These fits have seized a young man in my house, repeatedly; And lo! the spirit taketh him, and he suddenly *crieth* out, and *foameth* at the mouth, and gnasheth with his teeth, and is cast down wherever he may be seized, and pineth away until you would think he was actually dead. Matthew calls him a lunatic, but according to Mark it was a dumb spirit. And there are cases in which the disease accompanies, if it does not occasion, dumbness. The instance mentioned in Mark v. 2-16, and Luke viii. 26-36, was most remarkable, but there are some very similar at the present day, — furious and dangerous maniacs, who wander about the mountains and sleep in dens and caves. In their worst paroxysms they are quite unmanageable, and prodigiously strong. It is one of the most common traits of this madness that the victims refuse to wear clothes. I have often seen them absolutely naked in the streets of Beirût and Sidon. There are also cases in which they run wildly about the country, and frighten the whole neighborhood. It would certainly be rash to decide that this calamity is the work of evil spirits; and yet the manifestations are so inhuman and satanic, and the real causes so mysterious, that I am not much disposed to dispute the point with the natives of the country, who ascribe the mischief to supernatural agency."

Out of the Tombs. — Burckhardt speaks of finding in the immediate neighborhood where this miracle is supposed to

exceedingly fierce, so that no one could pass that way; and one of them had been possessed a long time, and wore no clothes, and could not be bound, not even with chains; for chains and fetters had often been put upon him, but he had snapped the chains asunder, and broken the fetters in pieces. And no man could master him; and always night and day, he was out in the mountains and in the tombs, crying out, and cutting himself with stones. But when he saw Jesus afar off, he ran to him, and, falling at his feet, cried with a loud voice, "Jesus, Son of the Most High God! I adjure thee by God, torment me not!" Jesus asked him, "What is your name?" for he was about to say to the foul spirit, "Come out of the man!" He answered, "Legion; for we are many." Now there was near, on the mountains, a great herd of swine feeding, and all

have occurred, the ruins of many large tombs. Some of them were natural caves, and others recesses hewn out of the solid rock, with cells on their sides for the reception of the dead, and often so large as to be supported with columns. They would thus afford ample shelter, and their tenants would not be molested, for the Jews regarded all such places as unclean. At the present day, the ruins of ancient tombs, are often resorted to for shelter by the Bedâwins.

A herd of Swine. — By the Law of Moses swine were unclean, and the touch of them, when dead, defiled a man; but the owner of this herd bred them, probably, for sale to the Gentiles. The eating of their flesh is generally supposed to cause cutaneous diseases in hot countries, and hence, among a people so liable to leprosy as the Jews, there was reason for its prohibition as food. It has been said that Jesus, by this miracle, caused a wanton destruction of property; but to this it may be answered that the owner of the swine, if a Jew, — and Josephus says there were multitudes

the demons earnestly entreated Jesus not to send them out of the country nor into the abyss, but into the herd of swine. He gave them leave immediately, and the foul spirits left the men, and went into the swine; and the whole herd — about two thousand — rushed violently down a steep place into the sea, and were drowned in the lake. And those that kept the swine fled, and told what had befallen them in the city and in the country. The inhabitants then went out to see what had been done; and coming to Jesus, they saw the possessed man — he that had the legion — sitting at his feet, clothed, and in his right mind. And those who had seen told them by what means the possessed man had been healed, and also how it was about the swine. Then all the people of the neighborhood besought Jesus to leave them; for they were seized with terror. And when he was going into the boat, the man out of whom the demons had gone, begged to go with him; but Jesus sent him away, saying, "Go home to your friends, and tell them what God, in his compassion, has done for you." And

of hellenistic Jews in that region, — deserved punishment for violating the Levitical Law. If he were not a Jew, what worse was the drowning of two thousand swine, than the sweeping off, by murain and the rhinderpest, of multitudes of cleaner brutes? and this Providence does at its pleasure.

Out of the Country. — It was the opinion of the Jews, as appears from Daniel x. 13, 20, that different evil spirits preside over distinct regions; and it is a superstition as old as man, that "ghosts" haunt the places of their earthly abode.

The Abyss. — It is a noticable fact that the demons whom Jesus expelled, expressed a dread of being sent into the "abyss," or of being "tormented before the time."

the man went, and published throughout Decapolis the great work that Jesus had done, and all wondered. And when Jesus had passed over again to the other side, many people gathered together, and received him gladly; for all were waiting for him.

And Matthew made Jesus a feast in his house, and a great company of tax-gatherers and others were there at table with him and his disciples. And the Scribes and Pharisees, seeing him eating with these tax-gatherers and sinners, said to his disciples, "How is it that he eats and drinks with tax-gatherers and sinners?" Jesus, hearing this, said to them, "The whole need not a physician, but those that are sick. Go you and learn what this means. 'I would have mercy, and not sacrifices.' I came not to call the righteous, but sinners to repentance."

Then came to him the disciples of John, saying, "Why, when we and the Pharisees fast often, do not your disciples fast?" Jesus said to them, "Can the friends of the bridegroom mourn, so long as the bridegroom is with them? But the days are coming when the bridegroom will be taken from them, and then they will fast. No one puts a piece of new cloth upon an old garment, for it will tear away

The Pharisees fast often.—They, and the more religious among the Jews, fasted twice a week; on Mondays and Thursdays. It appears that this discourse took place on Monday, and therefore Jesus gave especial offence to the Pharisees by feasting with tax-gatherers on a day when they held that a good man should fast.

New Cloth.—Undressed cloth fresh from the loom shrinks when it becomes wet, and then draws up and tears away from the old.

from the garment, and the rent will be made worse; nor do men put new wine into old skins; for the skins will burst, the wine run out, and the skins perish; but they put new wine into new skins, and both are preserved. Also, no one having drunk of old wine at once desires new, for he says 'the old is better.' *

While he was speaking these things, and many people were collected about him, there came one of the rulers of the Synagogue, named Jairus, who had an only daughter, about twelve years old, who lay dying. As soon as he saw Jesus he fell at his feet, and earnestly besought him, saying, "My little daughter lies at the point of death. Come, lay your hand upon her, and she will live."

Jesus went with the ruler, and so did his disciples, and a great multitude followed. And a certain woman who had a flowing of blood for twelve years, and had suffered much from many physicians, — spending all that she had without being bettered, but rather growing worse, — having heard of Jesus, came behind in the throng, and touched the fringe of his garment; for she said to herself, "If I but touch his garment, I shall be made well." And at once the

New Skins. — Goat skins are still used in eastern countries for holding and transporting liquids. They were common among both Jews and Romans. Those for wine had the hair on the inside, and the outside was coated with pitch; those for water had the hair on the outside. From long usage, the skins become tender, and swell and burst if filled with new wine, which soon ferments; so would it be, Jesus says, if his new truths were inclosed in the old system of the Pharisees.

Fringe of his Garment. — This was, no doubt, the square

* Matt. ix. 10-17. Mark ii. 15-22. Luke v. 29-39.

fountain of her blood was dried up, and she felt in her body that she was cured of her malady. Jesus, knowing immediately in himself that power had gone out of him, turned to the multitude and said, "Who touched my garment?" All denied having done so, and Peter and those with him, said, "Master, the people are thronging upon you, and do you ask 'Who touched me?'" Jesus said, "Somebody has touched me; for I perceive that power has gone out of me;" and he looked around to see who had done it. Then the woman, seeing that she was discovered, came to him trembling, and falling at his feet told, before all the people, why she had touched him, and how she had been healed immediately. And Jesus said to her, "Daughter, be of good comfort; your faith has made you whole; go in peace."

While he was thus speaking one came from the house of the ruler of the Synagogue, and said to him, "Your daughter is dead; trouble not the master." But when Jesus heard this, he said, "Fear not; only have faith, and all will be well." And when he came to the house he allowed no one to go in, but Peter and James and John, and the father and mother of the maiden. And the minstrels and the people were

garment worn over the shoulders, and called elsewhere a "cloak." It was surrounded by a fringe, and at its four corners were tassels of threads or strings. (See Numbers xv. 38, 39. Deut. xx. 11, 12.) This garment was peculiar to the Jews, and was worn to distinguish them from other nations.

The Minstrels. — The use of instruments at funerals was of heathen origin, and was not introduced until comparatively late among the Jews. These were professional minstrels, who were employed to mourn for the dead in a frantic

weeping and bewailing her, but he said, "Weep not; she is not dead, but sleeping." And they laughed in derision, knowing that she was dead. But, putting them all out, he took her by the hand, and said, "Maid, arise;" and her spirit came again, and she arose at once, and walked, and all were greatly astonished. But he charged them strictly that no one should know it, and directed that something should be given her to eat.*

When Jesus departed thence two blind men followed him, crying, "Son of David, have mercy on us." And when he had entered the house, the blind men came to him, and Jesus said to them, "Believe you that I am able to do this?" They said to him "Yea, Lord." Then he touched their eyes, saying, "According to your faith be it done to you." And their eyes were opened. Jesus strictly charged them to tell no one; but they, departing, spread it abroad in all that country. As they went out, a dumb man, possessed with a devil, was brought to him. And when the devil was cast out the dumb man spoke, and the multitude marvelled, saying it was never so seen in Israel. But the Pharisees said, "He casts out devils through the prince of devils."

And going out from thence with his disciples, he came into his own town, and on the Sabbath taught in the Synagogue, and many who heard him were astonished, and said, "Whence has this man these gifts? And what wisdom is this that is given him,

manner. As soon as one died the mourning began, and it was kept up until after the burial.

* Matthew ix. 18-26. Mark v. 22-43. Luke viii. 41-56.

that even such mighty works are wrought by his hand? Is not this the carpenter, the son of Mary, the kinsman of James, and Joses, and Judah, and Simon? And are not his kinswomen here with us?" And they took offence at him; but Jesus said to them, "A prophet is not without honor, except in his own town, and among his own kindred, and in his own family." But he could do no mighty work there, except laying his hands on a few sick people, and healing them; and he wondered at their unbelief.

And Jesus went through all the cities and villages, teaching in the synagogues, and preaching the glad tidings of the kingdom, and healing all kinds of sickness and diseases among the people. But when he saw the multitude, he said to his disciples, "The harvest truly is plenteous, but the laborers are few. Pray ye, therefore, the Lord of the harvest, to send forth laborers into his harvest." Then calling the twelve together he gave them power over all foul spirits, and all diseases, and sent them forth two by two, saying, "Go not away to the Gentiles, nor enter any city of the Samaritans. But go rather to the lost sheep of the house of Israel. And as ye go, proclaim that the kingdom of heaven is at hand. Heal the sick, cleanse the lepers, raise the dead, cast out demons; freely ye have received, freely give. Provide neither gold, nor silver, nor brass in your girdles, nor scrip for your journey, nor two coats, nor shoes, — but

Girdles. — Money was carried in a sack in the girdle which confined the outer garment or cloak.

Nor Scrip for your Journey. — The scrip was a leather bag hung about the neck, and used to carry food.

be shod with sandals,—nor staves, for the workman is worthy of his food. And in whatever city or town you may enter, inquire who in it is worthy, and with him abide till you go thence. And when you enter a house, salute it. And if the house be worthy, your peace will come upon it; but if it be not worthy it will return to you. And if any do not receive you, nor hear your words, when you depart out of that house, shake off the very dust of your feet for a testimony against them. Truly, I tell you, it will be more tolerable for Sodom and Gormorrah in the day of judgment than for that city. Lo! I send you as sheep into the midst of wolves; be therefore wise as serpents, and harmless as doves. Beware of men, for they will deliver you to the councils, and will scourge you in their synagogues. And you will be brought before governors and kings for my sake, that you may bear testimony to them and the Gentiles. But when they deliver you up, be not anxious how or what you

Nor Shoes.—The original word here in Matthew might be rendered sandals, if Mark did not say, "but be shod with sandals." The lower class of people commonly wore nothing on the feet; but in travelling sandals were necessary, and on long journeys, and in winter, a kind of short boot or shoe was worn. The meaning of the whole passage is that they were not to take forethought or make provision, as ordinary travellers would do.

Staves, are now always used by foot travellers over the rocky roads of Palestine, to support them in slippery places, and for defence against robbers; and it is usual, on long journeys, to take two lest one should fail.

Your Peace.—The Jewish form of salutation was "Peace be to this house." It is still retained among the Turks, and other eastern nations.

shall speak, for it will be given you in that hour what you shall speak; for it is not you who will speak, but the spirit of your Father who will speak in you. The brother will deliver up his brother, and the father his child, and children will rise against their parents, and cause them to be put to death; and you will be hated by all men for my sake; but he who endures to the end will be saved. When they persecute you in one city, flee to another, for truly I say to you, you will not have gone through the cities of Israel before the Son of Man will come. A disciple is not above his teacher, nor a servant above his lord. It is enough for the disciple to be as his teacher, and the servant as his lord. If they have called the master of the house Beelzebub, how much more will they so call those of his household. Fear them not, then, for nothing is covered which will not be revealed, nor hidden that will not be made known. What I tell you in darkness, preach in the light, and what is whispered in your ear, proclaim upon the housetops; and fear not those who kill the body, but are not able to kill the soul; rather fear Him who can destroy both soul and body in hell. Are not two sparrows sold for a farthing? and yet not one of them falls to the ground without your Father. The very hairs of your head are all numbered. Fear not, then, you are of more value than many sparrows. Whoever shall acknowledge me before men, him will I acknowledge before my Father in heaven. But whoever shall deny me before men, him will I also deny before my Father in heaven. Think not that I come to bring peace on the earth; I come not to bring peace, but a sword,—to set a son against his father, and a daughter against her mother, and a daughter-in-law against her mother-in-law, and to make a man's foes those of his own household. He who takes not his cross and follows me, is not worthy of me. He who loves his life, will lose it, and he who loses his life for my sake, will save it. He who receives you receives me, and he who receives me receives him who sent me. He that receives a prophet, because he is a prophet, will receive a prophet's reward; and he who receives a righteous man, because he is a righteous man, will receive a righteous man's reward. And whoever gives only a cup of cold water to one of my little ones, because he is my disciple, truly I say to you, he shall not fail of his reward."

And when Jesus had finished these teachings to his twelve disciples, he departed thence to teach and to preach in their cities. And the disciples went forth and preached that men should repent. And they cast out many demons, and anointed with oil many that were sick, and healed them.*

Now Herod, on his birthday, gave a great entertain-

He who takes not his Cross.—The condemned man was obliged to bear his cross to the place of execution. Jesus tells his disciples that they must be prepared to submit to a death of torture and ignominy. An impostor would not have promised such rewards to his followers.

Herod, Tetrarch of Galilee, and son of Herod the Great. Shortly after this event he was defeated by Aretas, with whom he was then at war, and this the Jews regarded as a just punishment for his execution of John. Shortly after the death of Jesus he was deprived of his government by the

*Matt. ix. 35-38; x. 1, 5, 42; xii. Mark vi. 6-13. Luke ix. 1-6.

ment to his lords and chief captains, and the principal men of Galilee. And the daughter of Herodias came in and danced before them, and pleased Herod and his guests so much, that Herod said to the damsel, "Ask of me whatever you will, and I will give it you;" and he affirmed with an oath, "Whatever you ask of me I will give, to the half of my kingdom." And going out, she said to her mother, "What shall I ask?" And her mother answered, "The head of John the Baptist." And coming directly with haste to Herod, she said, "I will that you give me in a charger, the head of John the Baptist." And the king was greatly troubled, yet on account of his oath, and the guests who were with him, he would not refuse her, but sent immediately one of his guards

Romans, and with Herodias was sent into perpetual banishment. The daughter of Herodias — Salome — is said to have met with a violent and untimely death.

The Chief Captains — were the commanders of a thousand men.

The Head of John. — Josephus attributes John's execution to Herod's fear of his fomenting sedition among the people. Probably John's announcement that the kingdom of heaven was at hand, — which by the Jews was understood to be a temporal kingdom, — had created much excitement, and a disposition to rise against the Roman power; therefore Herod would naturally regard him as a dangerous man, and one likely to bring him into difficulty with the Romans. He no doubt looked upon Jesus in the same light, and his remark, "It is John," etc., probably means that he thought him only another exciter of sedition — John the Baptist come back again. From these considerations it is likely that Herod really desired the death of John, and that the occurrence narrated in the text was a mere pretext for putting him out of the way.

with orders to bring the head of John. So the guard went and beheaded John in prison, and brought his head in a charger, and gave it to the damsel, and she gave it to her mother. And John's disciples when they heard of it came, and taking the body, laid it in a tomb, and then went and told Jesus.*

Now the fame of Jesus had spread abroad, and Herod, hearing of the works that were done by him, was much perplexed, and said to his attendants, "John I have beheaded; but who is this of whom I hear such things?" And some answered, "It is John risen from the dead;" and others said, "It is Elijah, who has reappeared;" others, "One of the old prophets has risen again." But Herod himself said, "It is John? He is risen from the dead!" and he desired to see Jesus.†

And the Apostles returned, and collecting about Jesus, told him of all they had seen and heard, and what they had taught. And he said to them, "Come apart by yourselves into some desert place, and rest awhile;" for many were coming and going, and they had no leisure, not even to eat. And they went privately in a boat over the sea of Galilee, to a desert place belonging to the city called Bethsaida. But

Desert place belonging to Bethsaida. — There was, it is supposed, a Bethsaida on the west of the lake, near to Capernaum and Chorazin, and probably, as the name denotes, close to the water's edge, and this place it is thought, was the native town of Andrew, Peter, and Philip. But there was also another town of the same name, — called Bethsaida Julius, —

* Matt. xiv. 6–13. Mark vi. 21–29.
† Matt. xiv. 1, 2. Mark vi. 14-16. Luke 14.

many saw and knew them as they were going, and ran together there on foot, from all the cities, and came before them, because they had seen the miracles he had done on those that were diseased. And Jesus, when he came out of the boat, saw the multitude, and was moved with compassion toward them, because they were as sheep without a shepherd; and going up into a mountain, he sat down with his disciples, and taught the people many things about the kingdom of God, and healed such as had need of healing.

And when the day began to wear away, his disciples said to him, "This is a desert place, and now the day is far gone; send the people away that they may go into the country round about, and into the villages, and buy themselves bread; for they have nothing to eat." Jesus answered, "They need not depart. Give them to eat;" but they said, "Shall we go and buy two hundred denaries worth of bread?" And he said to them, "How many loaves have you? Go and see." When

at the north-eastern extremity of the lake, and this was no doubt the scene of the miracle, for Luke says they crossed, after the event, "to Bethsaida, in the land of Gennesareth." The supposed scene of the miracle is a desert place, now called Buthiha, and is not far from the site of the town. At its south-east corner a bleak, barren mountain shuts down upon the lake, and the place is not capable of cultivation. A little cove is in its front, where boats could be moored, and a beautiful sward, on which five thousand could be gathered, crosses the foot of the rocks. The description of the locality agrees perfectly with the requirements of the Gospel narratives.

Two hundred Denaries. — About twenty-seven dollars; in those days a large sum, and probably more than the disciples had in their possession.

they were gone, he said to Philip, "Whence shall we buy bread, that these may eat?" This he said to try him, for he had determined what to do. Philip answered, "Two hundred denaries worth of bread would not be enough for every one of them to have a little." One of his disciples, Andrew, Simon Peter's brother, said to him, "There is a lad here who has five barley loaves, and two small fishes; but what are those among so many." Then Jesus said, "Make them all recline in companies of fifties, on the grass, and bring the loaves and fishes here to me." Now there was much grass in the place; so the men arranged themselves in ranks, by hundreds and fifties. And Jesus took the loaves, and looking up to heaven, he gave thanks, and distributed them to the disciples, and the disciples to those who were on the ground, and likewise of the fishes, as much as they desired. When all had eaten, and were satisfied, he said to his disciples, "Gather up the fragments that nothing be lost." Then they gathered them together, and filled twelve baskets with the fragments of the five barley loaves, and two small fishes which remained over and above after the people had eaten. And the number that had eaten was five thousand men, beside women and children. The multitude,

Barley Loaves. — Barley was only of about one third the value of wheat. The loaves were made thin and brittle, and were, therefore, broken and not cut.

Baskets. — It was customary for the Jews on a journey, to carry small flag baskets, slung over the shoulder, to hold their provisions, as there were then few inns, and they could not eat with Gentiles without pollution. Tacitus says that a flag-basket and a bundle of straw was the entire household furniture of a Jew.

when they saw this miracle said, "This is of a truth the prophet who was to come into the world." *

Then Jesus, perceiving that they were about to take him by force to proclaim him king, constrained his disciples to go before him to Bethsaida, while he withdrew to the mountains alone. And when it was evening, his disciples went down to the lake, and going on board the boat, set sail toward Capernaum; and the boat was in the midst of the lake, and Jesus alone upon the land. And he saw them toiling at the oars, for the wind was contrary, and the waves had risen by reason of a great wind that blew. And about the fourth watch of the night, when they had rowed five and twenty or thirty furlongs, Jesus went to them, walking on the sea; and when he drew near, they thought it was an apparition and cried out; for all saw him, and were terrified; but immediately he said, "Be of good cheer. It is I. Be not afraid."

Then Peter said to him, "Lord, if it be thou, bid me come to thee on the water." And Jesus said, "Come;" and Peter went down out of the boat, and walked on the water to go to Jesus; but when he saw the violence of the wind he was afraid, and beginning to sink, cried out, "Lord, save me!" And immediately Jesus stretched out his hand, and caught him, saying: "O thou of little faith, wherefore didst thou doubt." And he got into the boat with them, and the

About the Fourth Watch. — About three o'clock in the morning.

* Matt. xiv. 13-21. Luke ix. 10-17. John vi. 1-14.

wind ceased; and they were beyond measure astonished, and falling down at his feet said, "Truly, thou art the Son of God." They wondered, notwithstanding the miracle of the loaves; for they were slow of understanding.

Then they passed over and drew to the shore in the land of Gennesaret; and when they had left the boat the people heard of it, and ran at once through that whole region, and brought the sick in beds to the place where he was; and whenever he entered a village, or town, or hamlet, they laid the sick in the streets, and besought him to let them touch even the fringe of his garment, and all who touched it were made well.*

The day following the people who remained on the other side of the sea, knew that there had been only one boat there, and that Jesus had not gone on board of it with his disciples; but that they departed alone. But other boats from Tibereas, came near the place where they had eaten the bread, after the Lord had

The Land of Gennessareth — extended for about four miles along the west shore of the lake, and had an average breadth of about one and a half miles. It was a very fertile, thickly-settled plain, and in it were the towns Capernaum and Tiberias. Jesus appears to have landed not far from Capernaum; for he soon afterwards entered that town, (John vi. 24, 59).

Laid the sick in the Streets. — It was a very ancient custom to place the sick on the sides of thoroughfares, that the passers-by might communicate to them the remedies which had been useful to themselves in like cases. From this custom, it is said, arose the medical art.

Matt. xiv. 13-21. Mark vi. 45-56. John vi. 15-21.

given thanks. When, therefore, the people found that neither Jesus nor his disciples were there, they went on board these boats, and came to Capernaum, seeking Jesus.

And having found him on that side of the sea, they said to him, "Rabbi, when came you here?" Jesus answered them, "Truly, truly, I say to you. You seek me, not because you saw the miracles; but because you ate of the loaves and were filled. Labor not for the food which perishes, but for that which endures to everlasting life, which the Son of Man will give you; for on him the Father, even God, has set his seal."

Then they said to him, "What shall we do to work the works of God?" Jesus answered, "This is the work of God, that you have faith in him whom he has sent." Then they said to him, "What sign do you show that we may believe? What do you do, — our fathers ate manna in the desert, as it is written: 'He gave them bread from heaven to eat.'" Then said Jesus to them, "Moses gave you not the bread from heaven; but my Father is giving you the true bread from heaven; for the bread of God is that which is coming down from heaven; and giving life to the

What sign do you show. — On other occasions the Jews had asked for a sign from the visible heaven — which they supposed the dwelling of God, — thus showing that they expected some extraordinary physical phenomena would attend the coming of the Messiah. They now say to Jesus, in effect, "We have eaten of the loaves, — they were earthly food; but Moses gave us manna (bread) from *heaven* to eat. What like this do you do?" In view of this expectation his answer has peculiar force.

world." Then said they to him, "Lord, evermore give us this bread." Jesus said to them, "I am the bread of life; he who comes to me will never hunger, and he who believes in me will never thirst; but, as I have said to you, although you have seen me, you have not believed. All whom the Father gives to me will come to me, and he that comes to me, I will in no wise cast out; — for I came down from heaven not to do my own will, but the will of him who sent me. And this is the will of him who sent me, that of all he has given me I should lose none, but should raise every one in the last day. This I say is the will of him who sent me, that every one who sees the Son, and believes on him, should have eternal life. And I will raise him up at the last day." The Jews then murmured at him, because he said, "I am he who came down from heaven." And they said, "Is not this man Jesus, the son of Joseph, whose father and mother we know? How is it then that he says, 'I came down from heaven?'" Jesus therefore said to them, "Murmur not among yourselves. No man can come to me unless the Father who sent me, draw him, and him will I raise up at the last day. It is written in the prophets, "And they all shall be taught of God," every one, therefore, who hears, and learns of the Father, comes to me. Not that any one has seen the Father except he who is of God, he has seen the Father. Truly, truly, I say to you, he that believes on me has everlasting life.

"I am the bread of life. Your fathers ate the manna in the desert, and are dead; but if any man eats of the bread which comes down from heaven, he shall not die. I am the bread which came down from heaven;—if any man eat of this bread he shall live forever; and the bread that I will give is my flesh, which I will give for the life of the world." Then the Jews disputed among themselves, saying, "How can this man give us his flesh to eat?" And Jesus said to them, "Truly, truly, I say to you, unless you eat the flesh of the Son of Man, and drink his blood, you have no life in you. Whoever eats my flesh, and drinks my blood, has eternal life; and I will raise him up in the last day. For my flesh is meat indeed, and my blood is drink indeed. He who eats my flesh, and drinks my blood, abides in me and I in him. As the living Father has sent me, and I live by the Father; so he who eats me, will live by me. This is that bread which came down from heaven;—not as your fathers ate manna, and are dead;—he who eats of this bread will live forever."

These things Jesus said as he taught in the Synagogue at Capernaum. And many of his disciples, when they heard him, said, "This is a hard saying, who can listen to it?" But Jesus, knowing in himself that his disciples were murmuring at his words, said to them, "Does this give you offence? What then, if you should see the Son of Man ascend up where he was before? What is spiritual gives life, the flesh profits nothing, the words that I speak to you are spiritual, and they give life; but there are some of you who believe not,"—for Jesus knew from the beginning who they were that believed not, and who would betray him. And he said, "I told you that no man could come to me, unless it were given him from my Father."

From that time many of his disciples fell away, and went with him no longer. Then said Jesus to the twelve, "Would you also go away?" Simon Peter answered him, "Lord, to whom shall we go; you have the words of eternal life; we believe and are sure that you are the Holy One of God." Jesus answered, "Have not I chosen you twelve, and one of you is a slanderer?" He spake of Judas Iscariot, the son of Simon, for he it was who should betray him. After these things Jesus continued in Galilee, for he would not go into Judea, because the Jews sought to kill him.*

Is a Slanderer.—This is the common signification of the word in the original. It was used by the Jews, with the article prefixed, for Satan: but here the word lacks the article. And it is not probable that Jesus, though he knew Judas, would so early in his ministry have applied so harsh an epithet as "he hath a devil," to one whom he intended should continue with him to the end.

*John vi. 22-71; vii. 1.

PART FIFTH.

FROM THE THIRD PASSOVER, UNTIL THE FINAL DEPARTURE OF JESUS FROM GALILEE.

TIME — SIX MONTHS.

LIFE OF JESUS.

PART FIFTH.

THEN certain of the Scribes and Pharisees, who had come from Jerusalem, came to Jesus, and seeing his disciples eat with defiled, that is with unwashed hands, they found fault;—for the Pharisees and the Jews in general, holding the tradition of the elders, never eat without washing their hands. And on coming from market they do not eat without washing their bodies, and many other such observances they have, such as the washing of cups, and pots, and brazen vessels, and the couches for their tables. So the Scribes and Pharisees asked him, "Why do your disciples disregard the tradition of the elders; for they eat with unwashed hands?" He answered them, "And why do you, by your traditions, set aside the

Unwashed Hands.—On this subject the Pharisees were particularly scrupulous. The Talmud tells of a certain Rabbi, who, being confined in prison with only a small allowance of water, and having spilled a part, chose rather to die of thirst than to omit washing his hands with the remainder. It also says that "Whoever despises the washing of hands shall be rooted out of the world."

commands of God? Hypocrites! well do the words of Isaiah apply to you. 'This people honor me with their lips, but their hearts are far from me. But in vain do they worship me, teaching for truths the commandments of men.' For you neglect the commandments of God, and hold the traditions of men,— the washing of pots, and cups, and many such things. Ye do well! putting aside the commands of God, to keep your own traditions! Moses said, 'Honor thy father and thy mother, and whoever reviles father or mother let him die the death.' But you teach that a man may say to his father or mother, 'Whatever I have that might benefit you is Corban, (that is, a gift to God,) and you permit him to do nothing for his father or mother; thus making the command of God of no effect, through your traditions."

Then calling all the people to him, he said, "Hearken to me, all of you, and understand. Nothing which goes into a man from without, can pollute him; but what comes from him, that it is which pollutes the man. If any one has ears to hear let him hear."

Then his disciples came to him and said, "Know you, that the Pharisees were offended when they heard that speech?" But he answered, "Every plant which my heavenly Father has not planted, will be rooted up. Let them alone; they are blind leaders of the blind; and when the blind lead the blind, both fall into the ditch."

When he had left the people and entered the house, Peter and the other disciples, asked him concerning that dark saying. And he said to them, "Are you too. so dull of understanding? Do you not perceive that nothing from without, entering a man, can pollute him? For it enters not his mind, but his body, and its impurity is cast forth; but what comes from a man, that pollutes a man, for from within,—from the heart, come evil thoughts, adulteries, fornications, murders, thefts, covetousness, wickedness, deceit, lasciviousness, an evil eye, calumny, pride, madness. All these evil things come from within, and they pollute the man; but to eat with unwashed hands, pollutes not a man." *

Then Jesus departed thence, and went to the country about Tyre and Sidon. And entering a house, he would have remained unknown, but could not; for a certain woman,—a Gentile, a Syrophenician by nation,—whose daughter was possessed by a foul spirit, hearing of him, came forth to meet him, crying out, "Have mercy on me, O Lord, thou Son of David. My daughter is grievously troubled with a demon." But he answered her not a word, and his disciples came and entreated him to send her away, for she kept crying after them. He answered: "I am sent to only the lost sheep of the house of Israel." Then the woman fell at his feet, saying, "Lord help me." And he answered her, "It is not right to take the children's bread, and cast it to the dogs." But she said, "Truth, Lord, yet the dogs eat of the crumbs

Tyre and Sidon,—were on the shore of the Mediterranean, and not within the jurisdiction of Herod.

Syrophenicia,—was the name of the region about Tyre and Sidon.

Dogs,—was an epithet applied by the Jews to all Gentiles.

* Matt. xv. 1–20. Mark vii. 1–23.

which fall from their master's table." Then Jesus said to her, "O woman, great is your faith! Be it to you as you would. The demon has gone out of your daughter." And returning to her house, she found the demon gone out, and her daughter laid upon the bed.

Again, departing from the borders of Tyre and Sidon, Jesus returned to the sea of Galilee, through the midst of the Decapolis; and going up the mountain he seated himself, and great multitudes came to him, having with them those that were lame, blind, dumb, maimed, and many others; and they laid them down at the feet of Jesus, and he healed them. And all wondered when they saw the dumb speak, the lame walk, the blind see, and the maimed restored; and they gave glory to the God of Israel.

And one was brought to him who was deaf and had an impediment in his speech; and they besought Jesus to put his hand upon him. And taking him aside from the multitude he put his fingers into his ears, and spat and touched his tongue; and looking up to heaven and sighing deeply, he said to him "Ephphatha," that is, "be thou opened." And at once his ears were opened, and his tongue loosed, and he spoke plainly. And Jesus charged them to tell no one; but the more he charged them, the more a great deal they proclaimed it. And they were beyond measure astonished, and said, "He does all things well,—he makes both the deaf to hear, and the dumb to speak."

At this time, the multitude being very great, and

The evident intention of Jesus is to test the faith of the woman.

having nothing to eat, Jesus said to his disciples, "I have pity on the people, for they have now been with me three days, and have nothing to eat. If I send them home fasting, they will faint by the way; for some of them have come from far." His disciples answered "How in this desert place can we find food for so many?" And he asked, "How many loaves have you?" They said, "Seven." Then he directed the people to recline on the ground, and taking the seven loaves, he gave thanks, and broke, and distributed them to his disciples, to set before them. And they did so. And they had a few small fishes; and giving thanks, he directed that these also should be set before them. And the people ate till they were satisfied; and the disciples took up of the broken food that remained seven basketsful. And the number that had eaten was about four thousand, besides women and children. Then he sent them away, and taking a boat, went to the country about Magdala and Dalmanutha.*

Then the Pharisees, and also the Sadducees, came to him, and to try him, desired that he would show them a sign from heaven. He answered them, "In the evening, you say it will be fair weather, for the sky is red; and in the morning, you say it will be foul weather, for the sky is red and lowering. Hypocrites! You can read the face of the sky; but can you not

Dalmanutha and Magdala.—Dr. Lightfoot infers from Jewish writers that these were towns on the south-east side of the lake of Galilee.

* Matt. xx. 21–39. Mark vii. 24–37; viii. 1–9.

read the signs of the times?" And sighing deeply, he said, "Why does this race seek a sign? Truly I say to you no sign will be given to it, but the sign of Jonah the prophet." And he left them, and entering the boat again, departed to the other side.

Now the disciples, when they came to the other side, found they had forgotten to take bread, and had in the boat only one loaf. And he had charged them, saying, "Take heed of the leaven of the Pharisees and Sadducees." And they questioned among themselves, saying, "Is it because we have no bread?" Jesus, knowing this, said to them, "Why question you about the bread? Do you not yet perceive, nor understand? Are your minds still blinded? Having eyes, do you not see? and having ears, do you not hear? And do you not remember? When I broke the five loaves among the five thousand, how many baskets of fragments took you up?" They said to him, "Twelve." And when I broke the seven among the four thousand, how many baskets of fragments took you up? And they said "Seven." And he said to them, "How is it, then, that you do not understand that I spoke not of bread, when I bade you beware of the leaven of the Pharisees and Sadducees. Then they understood that he told them not to beware of the leaven of bread; but of the teaching of the Pharisees and Sadducees.*

And he went to Bethsaida, and they brought a blind man to him, and besought him to touch him. And taking the blind man by the hand, he led him out of the town, and wetting his eyes with spittle, he

* Matt xvi. 1-12. Mark viii. 10-21.

put his hands on him, and asked him if he saw anything. And he looked up and said, "I see men, as if they were trees, walking." Then he put his hands again on his eyes, and made him look up, and his sight was restored; and he saw them all clearly. Then Jesus sent him away to his house, saying, "Go not into the town, nor tell it to any one from the town." *

And Jesus, and his disciples went to the towns of Cesarea Philippi, and on the way, — when he was alone praying, — his disciples coming to him, he asked them, "Who do men say that I, the Son of Man, am?" And they answered, "Some say John the Baptist, others Elijah, and others Jeremiah, or one of the old prophets, risen from the dead." Then he said to them, "But who do *you* say that I am?" And Simon Peter answered: "Thou art the Christ, the Son of the living God." Jesus said to him, "Happy are you Simon, son of Jonah, for flesh and blood have not revealed this to you; but my Father in heaven; and I say to you, that you are Peter, and on this rock I will build my church, and the gates of Hades shall not prevail against it. And I will give to you the keys of the

Cesarea Philippi, — was situated at the foot of Mount Hermon and near the source of the Jordan. It is now called Banias, and is a wretched hamlet of about a hundred miserable huts, inhabited by Turks.

The gates of Hades. — The abode of the dead was thought, by both Jews and Gentiles, to be a subterranean receptacle, guarded by gates, from which there was no escape. Death was the entrance within these gates. The gates of ancient cities were the principal places where courts were held, and public matters deliberated on. By the gates of Hades are

* Mark viii. 22-26.

kingdom of heaven, and what you shall forbid on earth, will be forbidden in heaven; and what you shall permit on earth, will be permitted in heaven."

Then he charged them to tell no one that he was the Christ; and he told them also, how he must go to Jerusalem, and suffer many things from the elders, and chief priests, and Scribes, and be put to death, and raised again the third day. And he said this openly; but Peter took him to task, saying, "Be this far from you, Lord. This shall not come upon you." But he, turning about and looking at his disciples, rebuked Peter, saying, "Get ye behind me, Satan. You care not for the things of God, but for those of men." And calling together the people, with his disciples also, he said to them, "Whoever will come after me, must renounce himself, and take up his cross daily, and follow me; for whoever would save his life, will lose it; but whoever shall lose his life for my sake, and the Gospel's, he will save it. And what will it profit a man to gain the whole world, and lose his own soul? or what would a man give in exchange for his soul? Whoever shall be ashamed of me, and my words, among this apostate and sinful race, of him will the Son of Man be ashamed when he comes in the glory of his Father with his holy angels. Then he will reward every man according to his works. And truly I say to you, there are some standing here who will not taste of death till they have seen the Son of Man, coming in his kingdom." *

therefore meant the powers which were supposed to rule the rebellious invisible world.

Matt. xvi. 13-28. Mark viii. 27-37; ix. 1. Luke ix. 18-27.

And six days after these teachings, taking Peter and John and James, he went up into a high mountain to pray. And as he prayed, his countenance was transfigured and it shone like the sun, and his raiment became white as the light, and glistening. And two men talked with him, — Moses and Elijah, — who appeared in glory, and spoke of his departure, which was about to take place at Jerusalem. But Peter and those with him were overcome with sleep, and it was on waking that they saw his glory, and the two men with him. And as they were parting from him, Peter said to Jesus, "Master, it is good for us to be here, and, if thou wilt, let us make three tents, one for thee, and one for Moses, and one for Elijah;" for he knew not what to say. But while he was thus speaking, a bright cloud overspread them, and they were afraid when they saw the men enter the cloud. And there came a voice out of the cloud, saying; "This is my beloved Son in whom I am well pleased. Hear ye him." And when the disciples heard the voice, they fell on their faces, and were greatly afraid. But Jesus came and touched them, saying: "Arise, and be not afraid." And they lifted up their eyes, and looking round, saw no one but Jesus only.

As they were coming down from the mountain, Jesus charged them, saying, "Tell the vision to no one, till the Son of Man has risen from the dead." And they kept these words to themselves, questioning what the rising from the dead could mean. And they asked him, "Why do the Scribes say that Elijah must first come?" Jesus answered, "Elijah truly comes first, and reforms all things. But I say to you, Elijah has come already, and the people knew him not; but did to him whatever they would, as it was written of him; and so also, the Son of Man will suffer by them." Then the disciples understood that he spoke of John the Baptist, and they kept these things close, telling no one till Jesus had risen from the dead.*

On the next day when they came down from the mountain, he found a great number of people gathered about his disciples, and the Scribes disputing with them. And as soon as they saw him the whole multitude was struck with awe, and running to him, saluted him. And he asked, "What are you disputing about together?" And one of the multitude answered, "Master, I brought to you my son who has a dumb spirit, and when it seizes him, he foams at the mouth, and gnashes his teeth, and falls down insensible, and the demon bruises him, departing from him hardly, and leaving him utterly exhausted; and I besought thy disciples to cast him out, and they could not." Jesus answering said, "O faithless, and perverse generation! How long shall I be with you? Bring him to me." As he was coming, — as soon as he saw Jesus, the demon threw him down and tore him, and he rolled on the ground, foaming at the mouth. And Jesus asked his father, "How long has this been upon him?" And he said, "From a child; and often it casts him into the fire, and into the water to destroy him; and if you can do anything, have compassion on us, and help us." And Jesus said, "What means this, 'If you can?' All things are

*Matt. xvii. 1-13. Mark ix. 2-13. Luke ix. 28-36.

possible to him that believes." And at once the father of the child cried out with tears, "Lord, I believe; help thou mine unbelief." Then Jesus seeing the people murmuring together, rebuked the foul spirit, saying to it, "Thou dumb and deaf spirit, come out of him, and enter him no more." And crying out and rending him sorely, the spirit came out of the child; and he lay as one dead, so that many said "He is dead." But Jesus taking him by the hand, lifted him up, and he arose, cured from that very hour. And they were all amazed at the mighty power of God.*

When Jesus had entered a house, his disciples asked him privately, "Why could not we cast him out?" And he said to them, "Because of your unbelief; for truly I say to you, if you had faith as a grain of mustard seed, you might say to this mountain, 'remove hence to yonder place,' and it should remove, and nothing would be impossible for you. However, this race goes not out except by prayer and fasting."

And departing thence, they journeyed through Galilee, and he would that no man should know where he was; but while all were wondering at these works which he did, he said to his disciples, "Let these words sink into your ears; for the Son of Man is about to be betrayed into the hands of men. And they will kill him, and after he is killed, he will be raised again on the third day." But they understood not his words, and were afraid to question him.†

And when they had returned to Capernaum, the receivers of the tribute money came to Peter and said,

* Matt. xvii. 14. Mark ix. 14-29. Luke ix. 37-43.
† Matt. xvii. 22, 23. Mark ix. 30-32. Luke ix. 43-45.

"Does not your master pay tribute?" He said, "Yes." And on his return to the house, before he had spoken of it, Jesus said to him, "What think you Simon? Of whom do the kings of the earth take taxes or tribute money, of their own children, or of strangers?" Peter said to him, "Of strangers." Jesus said, "Then are the children free; but that we may not offend them, go to the sea and cast in a hook. Take the fish that first comes up, and on opening its mouth you will find a stater, that give to them for me and you." *

About this time there arose a dispute among the disciples, as to which of them should be greatest in the kingdom of heaven. And being in the house, Jesus asked them, "What was it you disputed about on the road?" They held their peace, but Jesus knowing their thoughts, took a little child and set him in the midst of them; and when he had taken him in his arms, he said to them, "Truly I say to you, unless you are converted, and become as little children, you will not enter the kingdom of heaven. Whoever humbles himself as this little child, is greatest in the kingdom of heaven; and who receives one such little child for my sake, receives me. And whoever receives me, receives him that sent me. And he that is least among you all, the same shall be the greatest.

Stater.—A Roman silver coin of the value of a shekel. The tribute was a half shekel, and the stater therefore was of sufficient value to pay for two persons. This tax was not paid to the Roman government; but to the Jews for the temple service.

*Matt. xvii. 24–27. Mark ix. 33.

If any one desires to be first, he will be last of all, and the servant of all. Whoever shall cause one of these little ones, who believes in me, to fall away from me, it were better for him that a millstone were hanged about his neck, and he were drowned in the depths of the sea. Take heed that you despise not one of the humblest of my disciples, for I say to you, that in heaven their angels always behold the face of my Father. The Son of Man has come to save what was lost. What think you? if a man has a hundred sheep, and one of them has gone astray, will he not leave the ninety and nine, and go upon the mountains to seek that which has gone astray? And if he find it, truly I say to you, he rejoices more over it than over the ninety and nine which went not astray. Even so it is not the will of your Father that one of the humblest of these should be lost."

John said to him, "Master, we saw one casting out demons in thy name, and we forbade him, because he followed not with us." But Jesus said, "Forbid him not. No one can do a miracle in my name, and speak evil of me; for he that is not against us, is for us. And whoever gives you a cup of cold water in my name, because you belong to Christ, truly, I say to you, he will not lose his reward."

A mill stone hanged about his neck. — This was a mode of capital punishment practised among the Greeks, and ancient Hindoos, and it is probable that it was in use in Syria. It is still one of the "institutions" of Turkey.

Their Angels. — It was a general belief among the Jews, that every person was attended by an angel, who was considered as his representative, and to whom he was supposed to have a personal resemblance. See Acts xii. 15. Hebrew i. 14.

Then Peter came to him, and said, "Lord, if my brother sin against me, how often shall I forgive him? Till seven times?" Jesus answered him, "I say not until seven times, but until seventy times seven. If your brother sin against you, go alone to him, and tell him his fault; if he hear you, you have gained your brother. But, if he will not hear you, go to him again, with one or two more, that by the testimony of two or three witnesses, every word may be confirmed. If he neglect to hear them, tell the matter to your whole body assembled; and if he disregard them, let him be to you as a heathen and a tax-gatherer.

"Therefore the kingdom of heaven has been compared to a certain king, who would settle accounts with his servants, and when he began the reckoning, one was brought to him who owed him ten thousand talents; but as he had not money to pay, his lord ordered him to be sold with his wife and children, and all that he had, for the payment of the debt. Then the servant fell down at his feet, saying, 'Lord, have patience with me, and I will pay you all.' Then the master had compassion on him, and forgave him the debt. But the same servant went out, and found one of his fellow servants who owed him a hundred denarii, and he seized him by the throat, saying, 'Pay me what you owe me.' Then his fellow servant fell

Ten thousand Talents. — The silver talent was worth $1,519.23. The sum, therefore, would be about fifteen millions of dollars.

To be sold. — It was the custom to sell debtors into slavery among many of the Eastern nations. For notices of its existence among the Jews, see 2 Kings iv. 1. Lev. xxv. 39-46. Amos viii. 6.

down, and entreated him, saying, 'Have patience with me, and I will pay you all.' He would not, but cast him into prison till he could pay the debt. Their fellow servants seeing what was done, were very sorry, and told their master all that was done. Then his master summoned him, and said, 'Thou wicked servant, I forgave thee all thy debt at thy entreaty. Shouldest not thou, too, have had pity on thy fellow servant, as I had compassion on thee?' And his master was angry, and delivered him to the tormentors, till he should pay all that was due to him. Even so will my heavenly Father do to you, if you from your hearts forgive not every one his brother." *

After this the Lord selected seventy other disciples also, and sent them, two by two, before him to every town and place where he was about to go; and he said to them, "The harvest truly is great, but the laborers are few. Pray then the Lord of the harvest, to send laborers into his harvest. Go your way. Lo, I send you as lambs among wolves. Carry neither purse, nor scrip, nor shoes, and salute no man by the

Salute no man by the way. — The customary salutations among Eastern nations are formal and tedious, and consume much time. If an Oriental meets an acquaintance, he stops, however urgent his business, to make and answer an endless number of inquiries; and to this delay the seventy were exposed, as they were doubtless going where they were known. To avoid a like waste of time they were forbidden to go "from house to house." It is still the custom in Palestine, when a stranger arrives in a village, for the neighbors to invite him to eat with them. The custom involves much ostentation and hypocrisy; but a failure to observe it is

* Matt. xvii. 1-35. Mark ix. 33-50. Luke ix. 46-50.

way. And whatever house you enter, on entering say, 'Peace be to this house.' And if one worthy of peace be there, your peace will rest upon it, if not, it will return to you again. Go not from house to house, but remain in the same house eating and drinking what they give, for the laborer is worthy of his hire. And in whatever town you are welcomed, eat what is set before you, and heal the sick who are there, and say to the people, 'The kingdom of heaven is at hand.' But in whatever town you are not welcomed, go out into the streets, and say, 'Even the dust which cleaves to our feet do we shake off against you; but be sure of this, the kingdom of heaven is at hand.' I say to you it will be more tolerable in that day for Sodom, than for that town; for he that receives you, receives to me, and he that rejects you, rejects me, and he that rejects me, rejects him that sent me." *

When the time was near, that he was to be received up, he steadfastly set his face to go to Jerusalem. And the Jews' festival of tabernacles being at hand, his kinsmen said to him, 'Depart hence and go to Judea, that your disciples there may see the works that you are doing. No one who would be known, does his works where they cannot be seen." For not even his kinsmen had faith in him.

Then Jesus said to them, "My time has not yet come; but all times are suitable for you. The world cannot hate you, but me it hates, because I testify of it, that its deeds are evil. Go you up to this festival,

strongly resented, and often leads to alienation and feuds among neighbors.

* Luke x. 1-11.

I am not yet going up, for my time is not yet fully come.'

Having said this he stayed behind in Galilee; but when his kinsmen had gone up, he also went to the festival, not openly, but as it were in a private manner, — sending messengers before, to make ready for him. And they entered a village of the Samaritans, *but the Samaritans would not receive him because they knew he was going to Jerusalem. And his disciples, James and John, when they knew this, said, "Lord, shall we call down fire from heaven, to consume them, even as Elijah did?" But he turned and rebuked them, saying, "You know not what manner of spirit you are of; the Son of Man is not come to destroy men's lives, but to save them." And they went to another village.

And on the way to Jerusalem, he passed through the confines of Samaria and Galilee, and was about to enter a certain village, when there met him ten lepers, who, standing afar off, cried out, "Jesus, Master, have pity on us." Seeing them, he said, "Go, show yourselves to the priests." And while they were going, they were cleansed. And one of them, seeing that he was healed, turned back, giving glory to God with a loud voice; and he fell on his face at the feet of Jesus, giving him thanks; and he was a Samaritan. Jesus said, "Were there not

There met him ten Lepers. — Lepers were excluded from towns, and these, therefore, met Jesus outside the gates of the village. From instances in Seneca it appears to have been a custom for sick people to cast themselves, on their recovery, at the feet of the physician, and embrace his knees.

* John vii. 2-10. Luke ix. 52-56; xxii. 11-19.

ten cleansed? Where are the other nine? Were there none to return, and give glory to God but this stranger?" And he said to him, "Arise, go your way; your faith has made you whole."

PART SIXTH.

FROM THE FESTIVAL OF TABERNACLES TO THE ARRIVAL AT BETHANY.

TIME — SIX MONTHS, LESS SIX DAYS.

LIFE OF JESUS.

PART SIXTH.

THE Jews sought Jesus at the festival, saying, "Where is he?" And there was much discussion among the multitude concerning him; some saying, "He is a good man," others, "Nay; he deceives the common people." However, no one spoke openly of him for fear of the rulers. Now, about the middle of the festival, he went up to the temple and taught; and the Jews wondered, saying, "How knows this man letters, having never learned?" Then Jesus said to them, "My teaching is not mine, but His who sent me. If any man will do his will, he will know of the doctrine, whether it be of God, or whether I speak from myself. He who speaks from himself, seeks his own glory; but he who seeks the glory of Him that sent him, he is true, and no iniquity is in him. Has not Moses given you the Law; yet none of you keep the Law. Why do you go about to kill me?" The people answered, "You are mad. Who goes about to kill you?" Jesus answered, "I have done one work at which you all marvelled. Moses gave you circumcision, — not that it is of Moses; but of the fathers, — and you circumcise a child on the Sabbath;

if a child be circumcised on the Sabbath, that the law of Moses may not be broken, are you angry with me for making a man every whit whole on the Sabbath? Judge not according to appearance, but judge righteously."

Then some of the people of Jerusalem said, "Is not this the man whom they seek to kill? but see, he speaks boldly, and they say nothing to him. Do the rulers indeed believe that he is the Christ? However we know this man whence he is; but when Christ comes, no one knows whence he is." Then Jesus cried aloud, as he was teaching in the temple, "Ye know me, and ye know whence I am; and I have not come of myself; but He who sent me is true; Him you know not, but I know him, for I am from him, and he sent me." Then they sought to seize him; but no one laid hands on him, for his hour had not yet come. But many of the people believed in him, and said, "When Christ comes, will he do more miracles than this man does?"

When the Pharisees heard that the common people murmured such things concerning him, they and the chief priests sent officers to seize him. Then Jesus said to them, "But a little while shall I be with you; for I go to Him that sent me. You will seek me and will not find me, and where I am, there you cannot come." Then the Jews said one to another, "Where will this man go, that we shall not find him? Will he go to the dispersed among the Greeks, and teach the

The dispersed among the Greeks. — The dispersed Jews who were scattered about in various places out of the limits of Palestine. These foreign Jews were held in contempt by those of Palestine, who arrogated to themselves great superiority from their residence in the Holy Land.

Greeks? What means this saying, 'You will seek me, and will not find me; and where I am, there you cannot come.'"

On the great day of the festival, Jesus stood and cried aloud, saying, "If any man thirst, let him come to me and drink. As the Scripture says, 'From him who believes in me, will flow rivers of living water.'" But this he spoke of the Spirit which those who believe on him should receive; for the Holy Spirit was not yet given, because Jesus was not yet glorified. Many of the people, hearing these words, said, "Of a truth, this is the prophet." Others, "This is Christ," and others, "Is Christ to come out of Galilee? Does not the Scripture say that Christ comes of the seed of David, and from Bethlehem, the town of David?" So there was division among the people concerning him. And some of them desired to seize him, but no one laid hands on him.

Then the officers returned to the chief priests and Pharisees, and they asked them, "Why have you not brought him?" The officers answered, "Never man spoke like this man." Then the Pharisees said to them, "Are you also deceived? Have any of the rulers, or the Pharisees believed in him. But this multitude that knows not the law are accursed." Nicodemus — he who came to Jesus by night, being one of them — then said to them, "Does our law condemn a man, before it hear him, and know what he has done?" They answered, "Are you, too, a Galilean? Search and see, for no prophet arises from Galilee." Then every one went to his own house, and Jesus passed out to the Mount of Olives.*

*John vii. 11-53; viii. 1.

Early in the morning he came again to the temple, and all the people gathering about him, he sat down and taught them. And the Scribes and Pharisees brought to him a woman taken in adultery, and placing her in the midst, they said, "Master, this woman was taken in adultery, in the very act. Now Moses, in the Law, commands that such should be stoned; but what say you?" This they said to try him, that they might have something of which to accuse him. But Jesus, stooping down, wrote with his finger on the ground; and when they continued asking him, he raised himself, and said, "Let him that is without sin among you, cast the first stone at her." And again stooping down, he wrote on the ground. Hearing this, and being convicted by their own consciences, they went out one by one, beginning at the oldest, even to the last, and Jesus was left alone, with the woman standing in the midst. Jesus then rising, and seeing none but the woman, said, "Woman where are your accusers? Has no one condemned you?" She answered, "No one, Lord." He said to her, "Neither do I condemn you. Go, and sin no more."

Again Jesus spoke to them, saying, "I am the light of the world. He who follows me will not walk in darkness, but will have the light of life." Then the Pharisees said to him, "You bear testimony to yourself, — your testimony is not true." Jesus answered, "Though I bear testimony to myself, yet is my testimony true; for I know whence I came, and whither I go; but you cannot tell whence I came, and whither I go. You judge according to the flesh, I judge no man; but if I should judge, my judgment would be true; for it would not be mine alone, but mine and the Father's who sent me. It is written in your law that the testimony of two witnesses is true. I am one that testifies of myself, and the father who sent me also testifies of me." Then they said to him, "Where is your Father?" Jesus answered, "You neither know me, nor my Father. If you knew me, you would know my Father also." These words he said while speaking in the treasury of the temple, but no one laid hands on him, for his hour had not yet come.

Then he said to them again, "I go my way, and you will seek me, and will die in your sins. Where I go, you cannot come." Then the Jews said, "Will he kill himself, that he says, 'Where I go, you cannot come.'" He said to them, "You are from below, I am from above; you are of this world, I am not of this world. Therefore I said to you, that you would die in your sins; for unless you believe that I am he, you will die in your sins." And they said to him, "Who are you?" Jesus answered, "Even the same that I said from the beginning. I have much to say and to judge of you; but he who sent me is true, and I speak to the world what I have heard from him." They understood not that he spoke to them of the Father. Then Jesus said to them, "When you have lifted up the Son of Man, then will you know that I am he, and that I do nothing of myself, but speak as my Father has taught me. And He who sent me is with me; he has not left me alone, for I do always those things that please him." As he was then speaking many believed in him.

Then Jesus said to those that believed in him: "If you continue in my word, then are you my disciples indeed. And you will know the truth; and the truth will make you free?" Some answered him, "We are Abraham's children, and were never in bondage to any one; how say you then, you will be free?" Jesus answered them, "Truly, truly, I say to you, whoever commits sin is the slave of sin. And the slave abides not in the house forever; but the Son abides forever. Therefore, if the Son make you free, you will be free indeed. I know that you are Abraham's children; but you seek to kill me, because my word has no place in you. I speak what I have seen with my Father, and you do what you have learned of your Father." They answered, "We are Abraham's children." Jesus said to them, "If you were Abraham's children, you would do the works of Abraham. But now you seek to kill me, a man who has told you the truth which he has heard of God; this did not Abraham. You do the deeds of your father." Then they said to him, "We were not born of fornication; we have one father, even God." Jesus answered, "If God were your Father, you would love me; for I came forth and am here, from God. And I have not come of myself, but He has sent me. Why do you not understand my speech? Because you cannot hear my word. You are of your father the devil; and the lusts of your father you will do. He was a murderer from the beginning, and abode not in the truth; for the truth is not in him. When he speaks a lie, he speaks from his own; for he is a liar, and the father of lies. Because I tell you the truth; you do not believe me. Who of you convicts me of sin? If I speak the truth, why do you not believe me? He that is of God, hears God's words. You hear them not, because you are not of God."

Then answered the Jews, "Say we not well, that you are a Samaritan, and have a demon?" Jesus answered, "I have not a demon; but I honor my Father, and you do me dishonor. But I seek not my own glory; there is one who seeks it, and will judge. Truly, truly, I tell you, if a man keep my words he will never see death." Then the Jews said to him, "Now we know that you have a demon. Abraham died, and the prophets died; and yet you say, if a man keep my words he will never taste of death. Are you greater than our father Abraham, who died? and the prophets, who died? Whom do you make yourself?" Jesus answered, "If I honor myself, my honor is nothing. It is my Father who honors me, and he, you say, is your God. Yet you know him not, but I know him; and if I should say I knew him not, I should be a liar like you; but I know him, and keep his word. Abraham, your father, rejoiced to see my day. And he saw it and was glad." Then said the Jews to him, "You are not fifty years old, and have you seen Abraham?" Jesus said to them "Truly, truly, I say to you, before Abraham was, I am." Then they took up stones to cast at him, but he hid himself, and went out of the temple.*

And going to the village called Bethany, a certain woman named Martha received him into her house; and she had a sister called Mary, who seating

* John viii. 12-59.

herself at Jesus' feet, listened to his words. But Martha was busily occupied with serving, and coming to him she said, "Lord, care you not that my sister leaves me to serve alone? bid her help me." Jesus answered her, "Martha, Martha, you are careful and troubled about many things, but one thing is needful; and Mary has chosen that better part, which will not be taken from her." *

And a certain teacher of the law came to him, and to try him, said, "Master, what shall I do to inherit eternal life?" Jesus said to him, "What is written in the law; what read you there?" He answered, "Thou shalt love the Lord thy God, with all thy heart, with all thy soul, with all thy mind, and with all thy strength; and thy neighbor as thyself." Jesus said to him, "You have answered rightly. Do this, and you will live." But he, wishing to justify himself, said, "Who is my neighbor?" Jesus answered, "A certain man went down from Jerusalem to Jericho, and fell among thieves; who, stripping him of his raiment, and wounding him, went away, leaving him half dead. And by chance a certain priest, going that way, saw him, and passed by on the other side; and

Down from Jerusalem to Jericho.—Jericho is in the valley of the Jordan, about fifteen miles from Jerusalem, and on considerably lower ground. The road between the two places passes through what is called the "Wilderness of Jericho,"— a rocky, mountainous region, sparsely inhabited, and still infested with robbers. Josephus says that at this time Judea was overrun with highwaymen, who committed the greatest excesses, and that this road was particularly dangerous.

* Luke x. 38-42.

also a Levite coming to the place, looked at him, and passed by on the other side. But a certain Samaritan on a journey, coming where he was, saw him, and taking pity on him, went to him, and bound up his wounds, pouring on oil and wine. And setting him on his own beast he carried him to an inn, and took care of him; and on the morrow he took out two denarii, and giving them to the inn-keeper, said, 'Take care of this man, and any further charge I will pay you when I come again.' Now which of these three, think you, was neighbor to him who fell among the thieves?" And he said, "He that took pity on him." Then said Jesus to him, "Go, and do thou likewise." *

He was praying in a certain place, and when he ceased, his disciples said to him, "Lord, teach us to pray, as John taught his disciples." Jesus said to them, "When you pray, say: Our Father who art in heaven, Hallowed be thy name, Thy kingdom come, Give us day by day our needful food, And forgive us our sins, for we forgive every one who sins against us, And bring us not into trial."

Then he said to them, "Suppose one of you should have a friend, and should go to him at midnight, and say, 'Friend, lend me three loaves, for a friend of mine has come to me in his journey, and I have nothing to

Go to him at Midnight. — It is customary in Eastern counties to travel at night, when it can be done safely, owing to the extreme heat of the days.

Lend me three Loaves. — It was usual among the Jews for neighbors to borrow bread of one another, and certain rules were laid down, when and on what conditions, it should be loaned.

* Luke x. 25-37.

set before him.' And he should answer from within: 'Trouble me not, the house is now shut; and I and my children are in bed. I cannot rise and give them to you.' I tell you, though he may not rise and give them because he is a friend, yet if the other importune him, he will rise and give him as many loaves as he needs. So, I say to you, Ask, and it will be given you; seek, and you will find; knock, and the door will be opened to you."*

The seventy returned with joy, saying: "Lord, even the demons are subject to us through your name." And he said to them, "I saw Satan fall as lightning from heaven. Lo! I give you power to tread on serpents, and scorpions, and over all the might of the enemy; and nothing shall at all injure you. But in this rejoice not—that the spirits are subject to you,—rather rejoice that your names are written in heaven."†

Jesus was at Jerusalem, at the festival of the dedication; and as he was passing along, he saw a man who had been blind from his birth; and his disciples asked him: "Who sinned, this man, or his parents, that he was born blind?" Jesus answered: "Neither did this man sin nor his parents; but that the works of God might be made manifest in him. I must work the works of Him who sent me while it is day; the night is coming when one cannot work. While I am in the world, I am the light of the world." Saying this, he spat on the ground, and making clay of the spittle, anointed with it the eyes of the blind man, saying to him, "Go, wash in the pool of Siloam,"—

The Pool of Siloam, was at the foot of Mount Zion, and

* Luke xi. 1-7. † Luke x. 17-20.

which word means sent. And he went and washed, and came back seeing.

Then the neighbors, and those who before had seen the man as a beggar, said, "Is not this he who used to sit and beg?" Some said "It is he;" others "He is like him;" but he said, "I am he." Then they said to him, "How were your eyes opened?" He answered, "A man called Jesus made clay and anointed my eyes, saying to me, 'Go to the pool of Siloam, and wash;' and I went and washed, and received my sight." Then they said to him, "Where is that man?" And he said, "I know not."

They brought to the Pharisees the man who had been blind. And it was on the Sabbath, that Jesus made the clay, and opened his eyes. Then again the Pharisees asked him how he received his sight; and he answered, "He put clay on my eyes, and I washed, and do see." Then said some of the Pharisees, "This man is not from God, for he does not keep the Sabbath." Others said, "How can a man who is a sinner do such things?" And there was a division among them. They spoke to the blind man again, and asked, "What say you of him who opened your eyes?" He said, "He is a prophet." But the Jews would not believe that he had been blind and received his sight, until they called his parents, and questioned them, saying: "If this be your son, and he was born blind, how then does he now see?" His parents answered, "We know that this is our son, and that he was born blind; but how he now sees we know not; nor do we

just outside the wall of the city. It is still shown to travellers.

know who opened his eyes. He is of age, ask him; he can speak for himself." This his parents said through fear of the Jews, for they had now agreed that if any one acknowledged Jesus to be the Christ, he should be put out of the Synagogue. Hence his parents said, "He is of age, ask him."

Then a second time the Pharisees called the man who had been blind, and said, "Speak in the fear of God. We know that this man is a sinner." The man answered, "I know not whether he be a sinner; but one thing I do know, that having been blind, now I see." Then said they to him again, "What did he to you? How did he open your eyes?" He answered them, "I have told you already, and you would not hear. Would you hear it again? Would even you be his disciples?" Then they reviled him, saying, "You are his disciple; but we are Moses' disciples. We know that God spoke to Moses; as for this man, we know not whence he is." The man answered, "Why, here is a strange thing, — you know not whence he is, and yet he has opened my eyes. Now, we know that God does not hear sinners; but if one worships him, and does His will, him he hears. Since the world began was it ever heard that a man opened the eyes of one born blind. If this man were not from God he could do nothing." They answered him, "You were wholly born in sin, and do you teach us?" And they thrust him out.

Jesus heard that they had cast him out; and finding

Put out of the Synagogue. — The person excluded from the Synagogue was not only prohibited from joining in public religious services, but was forbidden every kind of intercourse with others.

him, he said to him, "Do you believe on the Son of God?" He answered, "Who is he, Lord, that I should believe on him?" Jesus said to him, "You have seen him, and it is he who speaks to you." And he said: "Lord, I believe;" and worshipped him. And Jesus said, "For judgment I came into this world, that they who see not, may see, and that they who see may become blind."

Some of the Pharisees who were with him, on hearing these words, said, "Are even we blind?" Jesus said to them, "If you were blind you would not sin; but now, while you say, 'We see,' your sin remains. Truly, truly, I say to you, he who enters not by the door, but climbs into the sheep-fold some other way, he is a thief and a robber; but he who enters by the door is the shepherd of the sheep; to him the porter opens, and the sheep hear his voice, and he calls his sheep by name, and leads them out. And when he puts forth his own, he goes before them; and the sheep follow, for they know his voice; and a stranger they will not follow, but will flee from him, because they know not the voice of strangers." This parable spoke Jesus to them; but they understood not its meaning.

Again Jesus said to them, "Truly, truly, I am the door of the sheep. All who have come before me are thieves and robbers; but the sheep did not hear their voice. I am the door; whoever enters by me will be safe; and will go in and out, and find pasture. The thief comes only to steal, to kill, and to destroy; I have come that they may have life, and have it more abundantly. I am the good shepherd; the good shepherd lays down his life for the sheep. But the hireling, who is not the shepherd, whose own the sheep are not, sees the wolf coming, and leaves the sheep, and the wolf seizes them, and scatters the sheep. The hireling flees because he is a hireling, and cares not for the sheep. I am the good shepherd, and know my sheep, and am known by them. As the Father knows me, even so know I the Father; and I lay down my life for the sheep. Other sheep I have which are not of this fold; those also I must bring in, and they will hear my voice, and there will be one fold and one shepherd. For this my Father loves me, — because I lay down my life that I may take it again. No man takes it from me. I lay it down of myself. I have power to lay it down, and power to take it again. This charge have I received of my Father."

There was a division among the Jews, on account of these sayings; many of them saying, "He has a demon, and is mad; why hear you him?" others, "These are not the words of one who has a demon. Can a demon open the eyes of the blind?"

As Jesus walked in the temple in Solomon's porch, the Jews came about him, and said, "How long will you keep us in doubt? If you are the Christ tell us plainly." Jesus answered, "I have told you, and you do not believe. The works that I do in my Father's name bear testimony to me; but you believe not, because you are not of my sheep. As I told you, my sheep hear my voice, and I know them, and they follow me. I give them eternal life, and they shall never perish; nor shall any man pluck them out of my hand. My Father, who gave them to me, is greater than all; and no one is able to pluck them out of my Father's hand. I and my Father are one." Then again the Jews took up stones to stone him; but Jesus said to them, "Many good works have I shown you from my Father; for which of these do you stone me?" They answered, "For no good work do we stone you, but for blasphemy; because you, being a man, make yourself God." Jesus answered them, "Is it not written in your law, 'I said, Ye are gods?' If those are called gods to whom the words of God came, — and this Scripture cannot be set aside, — say you of him whom the Father has sanctified, and sent into the world, 'you blaspheme,' because he has said, 'I am the Son of God?' If I do not the works of my Father, believe me not. But if I do, though you believe not me, believe the works, and through them know that the Father is in me, and I in him." Then they sought again to take him; but he escaped out of their hands, and went away beyond the Jordan, to the place where John at first baptized, and there he remained. And many came to him there, who said, "John, indeed, did no miracle; but all that John said of this man is true." And many there believed in him.

Now a certain man was sick, — Lazarus of Bethany, the town of Mary and Martha. This Mary whose brother Lazarus was sick, was the same who *afterwards* anointed the Lord with ointment, and wiped his feet with the hair of her head. Then the sisters sent to Jesus to say, "Lord, lo! he whom you love is sick." Now he loved Martha, and her sister, and Lazarus; and on hearing this, he said: "This sickness is not to death, but for the glory of God, — that the Son of God may be glorified by it."

He remained two days in the place where he was; then he said to his disciples, "Let us go into Judea again." They answered, "Master, the Jews of late sought to stone you; and would you go there again?" Jesus answered, "Are there not twelve hours in the day? He who walks in the day stumbles not, because he sees the light of this world; if a man walk in the night he stumbles, because there is no light in him." This he spoke, and afterwards said, "Our friend Lazarus is sleeping; but I go to awake him out of sleep." Then said his disciples, "Lord, if he sleep, he will do well." Jesus spoke of his death; but they thought he had spoken only of taking rest in sleep. Then Jesus said to them plainly, "Lazarus is dead; and I am glad for your sakes that I was not there, that your faith may be confirmed. Let us go to him?" Then Thomas, who is called Didymus, said to his fellow disciples, "Let us also go, and die with him."

When Jesus came there, he found that Lazarus had already been in the grave four days. Now Bethany was near Jerusalem, about fifteen furlongs off; and many of the Jews had come to Mary and Martha, to comfort them for their brother. Then Martha, as soon as she heard that Jesus was coming, ran to meet him; but Mary sat still in the house. And Martha said to Jesus, "Lord, if you had been here, my brother would not have died. But I know that even now, whatever you ask of God, God will give you." Jesus said to her, "Your brother will rise again." Martha said to him, "I know that he will rise again, in the resurrection at the last day." Jesus said to her, "I am the

I know he will rise at the last day. — The Pharisees believed in the resurrection of the body at a general judgment.

resurrection and the life; he who believes in me though he should die, will yet live; and whoever lives and believes in me, will never die. Believe you this?" She said to him, "Yea, Lord, I believe that you are the Christ, the Son of God. He who was to come into the world." And when she had said this she called Mary, her sister, saying: "The Master is here, and calls for you." As soon as Mary heard this, she rose hastily, and went to him.

Now Jesus had not entered the town, but was in the place where Martha met him. The Jews then, who were with Mary in the house, comforting her, seeing her rise and go out, followed, saying: "She goes to the tomb to weep there." Then Mary, coming to where Jesus was, and seeing him, fell down at his feet, saying, "Lord, if you had been here, my brother would not have died." When Jesus saw her weeping, and the Jews who came with her, also weeping, he groaned in spirit, and was troubled. And he said, "Where have you laid him?" They said "Come and see." Jesus wept. Then said the Jews, "See how he loved him?" But some of them said, "Could not he who opened the eyes of the blind have saved this man from death?"

Jesus, still groaning in himself, came to the grave. It was a cave, and a stone lay upon it. Jesus said, "Take away the stone." Martha, the sister of the man who was dead, said to him, "Lord, by this time the body is offensive, for he has been dead four days."

A Cave is still shown as being the tomb occupied by the body of Lazarus. It is of only doubtful authenticity. It is, however, a most striking fact, that Bethany now bears his name, being called, *el-Azarîyeh or Lazarieh.*

Jesus said to her, "Did I not tell you that if you would believe, you should see the glory of God?" Then they took away the stone, and Jesus, raising his eyes to heaven, said: "Father, I thank thee that thou hast heard me, and I know that thou hearest me always; but I speak thus because of the people who are standing round; that they may believe that thou hast sent me." Having said this, he cried with a loud voice, "Lazarus, come forth!" And the dead man came forth, bound hand and foot with grave clothes; and his face bound about with a napkin. Jesus said to them, "Loose him, and let him go." Then many cf the Jews who came with Mary, and saw what Jesus had done, believed on him; but some of them went to the Pharisees, and told what Jesus had done.*

Then the chief priests and Pharisees held a council, saying: "What are we to do? This man is doing many wonderful works; and if we let him alone, all the people will believe in him, and the Romans will come and take away both our place and nation." But one of them named Caiaphas, who was High Priest that year, said to them, "You know nothing at all; nor do you consider that it is better for us that one man should die for the people, than that the whole nation should be destroyed." This he said not from himself, but, being High Priest that year, he prophesied that Jesus was about to die for the nation; and not for the nation only, but to bring together, in one body, the children of God wherever scattered. Then from that day they took counsel together, how to put him to death. Jesus, therefore, no longer appeared openly

* John xi. 1-46.

among the Jews, but went to the country near the desert, to a town called Ephraim, and there continued with his disciples. And great multitudes resorted to him there, and he healed them; and, as he was wont, taught them also.*

And in one of the Synagogues, in which he was teaching on the Sabbath, there was a woman who had been afflicted with a spirit of infirmity for eighteen years, and was bowed together, and unable to raise herself. When Jesus saw her he called her to him, and said, "Woman, you are freed from your infirmity." And he laid his hands on her, and immediately she stood up, and gave glory to God; but the ruler of the Synagogue, being angry because Jesus had done this on the Sabbath, said to the people: "There are six days in which people can work; therefore, in them come and be healed, and not on the Sabbath." The Lord then answered him, "Hypocrite! Does one of you on the Sabbath not loose his ox, or his ass from the stall, and lead him away to watering? And should not this woman — a daughter of Abraham, — whom Satan has bound, lo! these eighteen years, be loosed from this bond on the Sabbath day?" When he said this his opposers were ashamed. And all the people rejoiced for all the glorious things he was doing.†

As Jesus was going through the cities and villages teaching, on his way to Jerusalem, one said to him: "Lord, will only a few be saved?" And he said to them, "Strive to enter at the strait gate; for

*John xi. 47-54. Mark x. 1.
†Luke xiii. 10-17.

many, I say to you, will seek to enter and will not be able. When once the master of the house has risen, and shut to the door, you will stand without and knock, saying, 'Lord, Lord, open to us,' and he will answer you, 'I know not whence you are.' Then will you say, "We have eaten and drunk in thy presence, and thou has taught in our streets.' But he will answer, 'I tell you, I know not whence you are. Depart from me, all you workers of iniquity.' There will be weeping and gnashing of teeth when you see Abraham, and Isaac, and Jacob, and all the prophets, in the kingdom of God, and are yourselves shut out. And men will come from the east, and the west, and the north, and the south, and take places at table in the kingdom of heaven; and those who are first will be last, and those who are last will be first."

The same day certain Pharisees came to him, saying, "Go away from here, for Herod designs to kill you." He said to them, "Go, and tell that fox, Lo! I cast out demons and do cures, to-day and to-morrow, and on the third day my work will be finished. But I must work to-day, and to-morrow, and the day following; for it cannot be that a prophet should perish out of Jerusalem." *

He went into the house of one of the chief Pharisees to eat on the Sabbath, and those present were watching him. And lo! a certain man who had a dropsy came to him, and Jesus said to the teachers of the law and the Pharisees, "Is it lawful to cure on the Sabbath?" But they held their peace; and taking the man, he healed him, and letting him go,

* Luke xiii. 22-35.

said to them, "Is there any one of you, who, if his ass or his ox should fall into a pit on the Sabbath, would not at once draw him out?" And they could make him no answer to these words.

Observing how those who were bidden chose out the highest places at the table, he spoke a parable to them, saying: "When you are asked by any one to a wedding do not take the highest place; lest one more deserving of honor than you be bidden, and he that bade you should come, and say, 'Give this man place,' and you with shame have to take a lower seat. But when you are bidden take the lowest place; that when he who bade you come, he may say to you, "Friend, go up higher." Then you will be honored in the presence of the other guests. For, whoever exalts himself will be humbled, and he who humbles himself will be exalted." Then he said also to him who had invited him, "When you make a dinner or a supper, ask not your friends, nor your brethren, nor your kinsmen, nor your rich neighbors; lest they ask you in return, and you be repaid. But when you make a feast, invite the poor, the maimed, the lame, and the blind, and you will be blessed; for they cannot repay you; but you will be repaid in the resurrection of the just."

On hearing this, one of the guests said, "Blessed is he who shall eat bread in the kingdom of God." Jesus said to him, "A certain man made a great feast, and at supper time he sent his servant to say to those who were bidden, 'Come, for all things are now ready.' But with one accord they all began to make excuses. The first said to him, 'I have bought a piece of ground, and must go and see it. I pray you, have me excused.' Another said, 'I have bought five yoke of oxen, and go to try them. I pray you, have me excused.' And another said, 'I have married a wife; and therefore I cannot come.' So, the servant returned and told his lord what they said. The master, being angry, said to his servant, "Go out quickly into the streets and lanes of the city, and bring here the poor, the maimed, the lame, and the blind." Afterward, the servant said to him, 'Lord, it is done as you commanded; and yet there is room.' His lord said to him, 'Go out now into the highways and hedges, and constrain all you find to come in, that my house may be full; for, I say to you, that none of those who have been bidden shall taste of my supper."

And great multitudes were following him, and he turned and said to them, "If any man come to me and hate not his father, and mother, and wife, and children, and brothers and sisters, yea, and his own life also, he cannot be my disciple. And whoever does not follow me, bearing his cross daily, cannot be my disciple. Which of you, building a tower, sits not down first and counts the cost, whether he have enough to finish it? lest having laid the foundation, and not being able to finish, all who look on should mock him, saying: 'This man began to build, and was not able to finish.' Or what king going to war with another king, sits not down first and consults whether he with ten thousand, will be able to meet the one who comes against him with twenty thousand? If not, while the other is still at a great distance, will he not send an embassy, and sue for peace? No one of you who does not renounce all that he has, can be my disciple. He that has ears to hear let him hear." *

Then all the tax-gatherers and sinners drew near to hear him; and the Pharisees and Scribes murmured, saying: "This man receives sinners and eats with them." And he spoke to them in a parable, saying: "Who of you having a hundred sheep, should he lose one of them, does not leave the ninety and nine in the wilderness, and go after the lost one until he find it: and having found it, does he not lay it on his shoulders rejoicing? And when he comes home, does he not call together his friends and neighbors, saying, 'Rejoice with me, for I have found my sheep which was lost.' I tell you, that thus there is joy in heaven over one sinner that repents, more than over ninety and nine just persons, who need no repentance. Either what woman having ten pieces of silver, if she lose one piece, does not light a lamp, and sweep the house, and seek carefully till she find it? and having found it, does she not call her friends and neighbors together, saying: 'Rejoice with me; for I have found the piece I had lost.' Thus I tell you, There is joy among the angels of God over one sinner that repents."

He said also, "A certain man had two sons; and the younger of them said to his father, 'Father, give me

Light a Lamp. — Houses in the East were so badly lighted that to find a small object it would be necessary to use a lamp even in the day time. This is shown from the relics of Herculanean and Pompeii, where the smaller houses have no windows at all, and in such larger ones as have them they are only loopholes.

* Luke xiv. 25-33.

the portion of the estate that falls to me.' And he divided between them his living. And not many days after, the younger son, gathering all together, took a journey to a far country, and there wasted his property in dissolute living. But when he had spent all, there was a great famine in that country, and he began to be in want. And for support he attached himself to a citizen of that country, who sent him into his fields to feed swine. And he longed to fill himself with the pods that the swine ate: but no one gave him any. When he came to himself, he said, 'How many hired servants of my father have food enough, and to spare, while I am perishing here with hunger. I will arise and go to my father, and say to him: "Father, I have sinned against heaven and against you; I am no longer worthy to be your son: make me one of your hired servants."' And he set out to go to his father; but, while he was yet a great way off, his father saw him, and had pity on him, and ran, and fell on his neck, and kissed him. But the son said to him: 'Father, I have sinned against heaven, and against you, and am no longer worthy to be your son.' But the father said to his servants, 'Bring out the best robe and put it on him; and put a ring on his hand, and sandals on his feet; and bring the fatted calf, and kill it, and let us eat and be merry; for this my son was dead, and is alive again; was lost, and is found.' And they began to make merry. His elder son was in

To feed Swine. — This was looked upon as a most degrading and contemptible employment.

The best robe. — A long garment never worn by servants. Rings and shoes were also articles worn only by the better classes.

the field; and as he drew near to the house, he heard the music and dancing, and calling one of the servants, he asked what it meant. The servant told him, 'Your brother has come, and your father has killed the fatted calf; because he has received him safe and sound.' And he was angry, and would not go in. Then his father went out to entreat him; but he said to his father, 'Lo! these many years have I served you, and never transgressed your commands, and yet you never gave me a kid that I might feast with my friends; but as soon as this your son came, who has wasted your substance with harlots, you have killed for him the fatted calf.' Then his father said to him, 'Son, you are always with me, and all that I have is yours; but it was right to make merry, and be glad; for this your brother was dead, and is alive again, was lost, and is found.'" *

Jesus said also to his disciples, "A certain rich man had a steward who was accused of wasting his goods; and he sent for him, and said to him: 'What is this I hear of you? Give an account of your stewardship; for you can be no longer steward.' Then the steward said to himself, 'What shall I do, now that my lord takes away my stewardship? I cannot dig, to beg I am ashamed. I am resolved what to do, that when I am put out of the stewardship others may receive me into their houses.' So he called to him every one of his lord's debtors, and said to the first, 'How much do you owe my lord?' And he said, 'A hundred measures of oil.' Then he said to him, 'Take your contract, and sit down at once, and write fifty.'

* Luke xv. 1-32.

Then he said to another, 'And how much do you owe?' He said, 'A hundred measures of wheat.' And he said to him, 'Take your contract and write fourscore.' The lord commended the unjust steward for acting with forethought; and the children of this world, show more wisdom in their dealings than the children of light. And I say to you, make to yourselves friends with the riches of this world, so that when you fail they may welcome you to everlasting habitations.

"He who is faithful in what is least, will be faithful also in much. And he who is unjust in the least, will be unjust also in much. If, then, you are not faithful in the riches of this world; who will commit to your trust the true riches? And if you are not faithful in that which is another man's; who will give you that which is your own." *

And the Pharisees, who were covetous, heard all this, and they derided him. He said to them, "You make yourselves appear righteous before men; but God knows your hearts; and what is highly esteemed among men, is an abomination in the sight of God.

"There was a certain rich man who was clothed in purple and fine linen, and fared sumptuously every day. And there was a beggar named Lazarus, who was laid at his gate, covered with sores, and desiring to be fed with the crumbs which fell from the rich man's table; and even the dogs came and licked his sores. And the beggar died, and was carried by angels to Abraham's bosom. The rich man also died and was buried, and in Hades he lifted up his eyes,

* Luke xiv. 1-13.

being in torment, and saw Abraham afar off, and Lazarus in his bosom. And he called out to him, saying: 'Father Abraham, have pity on me, and send Lazarus to dip the end of his finger in water, to cool my tongue; for I am tormented in this flame.' But Abraham said, 'Son, remember that thou in thy lifetime didst receive good things as Lazarus received evil things; but now he is comforted, and thou art tormented. And besides all this, there is between us and you, a great gulf, so that those who would pass from us to you cannot, neither can those pass to us who would come from you.' Then the rich man said, 'I pray thee, Father, that thou would'st send him to my father's house, for I have five brothers, to bear testimony to them; that they also may not come to this place of torment.' Abraham said to him, 'They have Moses and the Prophets, let them hear them.' But he said, 'Nay, father Abraham; but if one should go to them from the dead they would repent.' Abraham said to him, 'If they hear not Moses and the Prophets, they would not be persuaded even though one rose from the dead.'" *

Then the apostles said to the Lord, "Increase our faith." And the Lord said, "If you had faith as a grain of mustard seed, you might say to this Sycamine tree, 'Be thou plucked up by the root, and planted in the sea,' and it would obey you; but which of you having a servant ploughing or feeding cattle would say to him, when he came from the field, 'Come, place yourself at table.' Would he not rather say to him, 'Make ready my supper, gird yourself, and serve

* Luke xvi. 19-31.

me till I have eaten and drunken, and then you shall eat and drink?' Would he thank that servant for doing as he had been commanded? I think not. Thus, when you have done all you are commanded, you should say, 'We are unprofitable servants, we have done only what was our duty to do.'" *

On being asked by the Pharisees when the kingdom of God should come, Jesus answered, "The kingdom of God comes not in outward appearance; nor will men say Lo! it is here! or Lo! it is there! for the kingdom of God is within you." And he said to his disciples, "The time will come when you will desire to see one of the days of the Son of Man, and will not see it. And men will say, Lo! he is here! and Lo! he is there! but go not forth, nor follow them. For the day of the Son of Man will be like the lightning which flashes over the whole heaven; but he must first suffer much, and be rejected by this generation. As it was in the days of Noah, so will it be in the days of the Son of Man. Men were eating and drinking, marrying and giving in marriage, until the day when Noah entered the ark, and the flood came, and destroyed them all. So, also, as it was in the days of Lot; they were eating and drinking, buying and selling, planting and building; but the same day that Lot left Sodom it rained fire and brimstone from heaven, and destroyed them all. Even so will it be at the coming of the Son of Man. Then let him who is on the housetop not come down to take anything out of his house; and let him who is in the field not turn back. Remember Lot's wife. Whoever shall

* Luke xvii. 5–10.

seek to save his life, will lose it, and whoever shall lose his life, will save it. I tell you, in that night there will be two in one bed; one will be taken, the other will be left. Two women will be grinding together; the one will be taken, and the other left. Two men will be in the field; the one will be taken, the other left." And they said to him "Where Lord?" And he answered them, "Wherever the body is, there the eagles will gather together." *

And he taught his disciples by a parable that men ought to pray always, and not to faint, saying: "There was in a certain city a judge, who feared not God, nor regarded man; and there was a widow in the same city, who came to him, saying, 'Avenge me on him who has wronged me.' He would not for a time; but afterwards he said to himself, 'Though I neither fear God, nor regard man; yet, as this widow troubles me, I will avenge her; that by her continual coming she may not weary me.' And the Lord said, 'Hear what the unjust judge determined.' And will not God avenge his own chosen who cry to him day and night, though he delay long in their cause? I tell you he will avenge them speedily. But when the Son of Man comes will he find this faith in the land?"

To some who trusted in themselves, thinking that they were righteous, and despised others, he spoke this parable: "Two men went up to the temple to pray; the one a Pharisee, the other a tax-gatherer. The Pharisee stood, and prayed thus within himself, 'O, God, I thank thee that I am not like other men; extortioners, unjust, adulterers; or even like this tax-

* Luke xvii. 20-37.

gatherer. I fast twice in the week, I give tithes of all I possess.' But the tax-gatherer, standing afar off, would not so much as lift his eyes to heaven, but smote on his breast, saying, 'God, be merciful to me a sinner.' I tell you, that this man went down to his house approved rather than the other. For he who exalts himself, will be humbled; and he who humbles himself, will be exalted.*

The Pharisees came to him, and to ensnare him, asked, "Is it lawful for a man to put away his wife, for whatever cause he will?" He answered them, "Have you not read, that the Creator in the beginning made a male and a female? And, it is said, For this cause a man shall leave father and mother, and cleave to his wife, and the two shall be one. So, they are no longer two, but one. What, then, God has joined together, let not man put asunder." They said to him, "Why, then, did Moses allow a writing of divorcement to put the wife away?" He said to them, "Moses, because of your hardness of heart, allowed you to put away your wives; but in the beginning it was not so. And, I say to you, whoever puts away his wife, except for adultery, and marries another, commits adultery. And whoever marries her who is put away, commits adultery."

And when they were in the house, his disciples said to him, "If the case of a man be such with his wife, it is better not to marry." He said to them, "All men are not capable of this, only those to whom it is given. There are eunuchs who are so from their birth, and there are eunuchs who are made so by men; and

* Luke xviii. 1-14.

there are those who have made themselves eunuchs for the sake of the kingdom of heaven. Let him who is able to receive this, receive it." *

Then young children were brought to him, that he might put his hands on them, and pray. And his disciples rebuked those who brought them. But when Jesus knew it he was much displeased, and said, "Let little children come to me, and forbid them not; for of such is the kingdom of heaven. Truly, I say to you, whoever does not receive the kingdom of heaven as a little child will not enter therein." And he took them in his arms, put his hands upon them, and blessed them.†

And when he had gone forth, a certain ruler came, running and kneeling to him in the road, who said, "Good Master, what shall I do to inherit eternal life?" And Jesus said to him, "Why call you me good? There is none good, but one, that is God. But if you would enter into life, keep the commandments." He said to him, "Which?" Jesus said, "These; thou shalt do no murder; Thou shalt not commit adultery; Thou shalt not steal; Thou shalt not bear false witness; Honor thy father and thy mother; and Thou shalt love thy neighbor as thyself." The young man said to him, "All these have I kept from my youth. What lack I yet?" Then Jesus, looking on him, loved him, and said, "If you would be perfect, go, sell what you have and give to the poor, and you shall have treasure in heaven; and then come, take up the cross, and be my disciple." The young man was sad at these words,

* Matt. xix. 3-12. Mark x. 2-12.

† Matt. xix. 13-15. Mark x. 13-16. Luke xviii. 15-17.

and went away sorrowful, for he had great possessions.

Then Jesus, looking round about, said to his disciples: "How hard it is for a rich man to enter the kingdom of God." And the disciples were astonished at these words; but Jesus said again, "Children, how hard it is for those who have riches to enter the kingdom of God. It is easier for a camel to go through the eye of a needle, than for a rich man to enter the kingdom of God." His disciples were astonished out of measure, and said among themselves, "Who then can be saved?" But Jesus, fixing his eye on them, said, "To men this would be impossible; but to God all things are possible."

Then Peter said to him, "Lo! We have forsaken all to follow you. What, then, will be our reward?" Jesus said to them, "Truly, I tell you, that you, who have followed me in the regeneration, when the Son of Man shall sit on the throne of his glory, shall also sit on twelve thrones, ruling the twelve tribes of Israel. And every one who has given up houses, or brothers, or sisters, or father, or mother, or wife, or children, or lands for my sake, shall receive a hundred fold, and inherit eternal life." *

"But many who are first will be last, and last will be first. For the kingdom of heaven is like a householder who went out early in the morning to hire laborers for his vineyard. And having agreed with them for a denarius a day, he sent them into the vineyard. And going out about the third hour, he saw others standing idle in the market-place, and he said to them, "Go you also into my vineyard, and

* Matt. xix. 16-30. Mark x. 17-31. Luke xviii. 18-30.

whatever is right, I will give you." And they went; and he went out again about the sixth and the ninth hour, and did the same. And about the eleventh hour, going out again, he found others standing idle, and said to them, "Why stand you here all the day idle?" They answered, "Because no one has hired us." He said to them, "Go you also into my vineyard, and whatever is right you shall receive." Then, in the evening, the lord of the vineyard said to his steward, "Call the laborers and give them their wages, beginning with the last and going to the first." And when they came, those who were hired about the eleventh hour received every one a denarius. So, when the first came they supposed they should receive more; but they also received every one a denarius. And when they had received it, they murmured against the good man of the house, saying, "These last have worked only one hour, and you have made them equal to us, who have borne the burden and heat of the day." But he answered one of them, "Friend, I do thee no wrong. Did you not agree with me for a denarius? Take what is yours, and go; I will give to the last, the same as to you. May I not do what I will with my own? Is your eye evil because I am good?" Thus the last will be first, and the first last; and many are called, but few are chosen." *

And they were on the road going up to Jesusalem, and Jesus was leading the way, and they were astonished, and followed him in fear. And, taking the twelve apart in the road, he told them what was about to befall him, saying, "Lo! we are going up to Jerusa-

* Matt. xx. 1-16.

lem, and all that has been written by the prophets concerning the Son of Man, will be fulfilled. For he will be delivered to the chief priests, and the teachers of the law; and they will condemn him to death, and deliver him to the Gentiles; who will mock him, and scourge him, and spit upon him, and crucify him, and the third day he will rise again." And the meaning of this was hidden from them; so they understood nothing of what he said.*

After this the mother of Zebedee's children came to him with her sons, and, falling down before him, they asked of him a favor. And he said, "What would you that I should do for you?" She said to him, "Grant that these my two sons may sit, the one on your right hand, the other on your left, in your kingdom." But Jesus answered her, "You know not what you ask. Can you drink of the cup that I drink of, and be baptized with the baptism that I am baptized with?" They said to him, "We can." Then he said to them, "You shall indeed drink of my cup, and be baptized with the baptism that I am baptized with; but to sit on my right hand, and on my left, is not mine to give; but it shall be given to them for whom it is prepared by my Father."

And when the ten heard of this they were angry with the two brothers. Jesus called them to him, and said, "You know that the rulers of the Gentiles lord it over them, and their great men have them under authority. It must not be so with you. But whoever would be great among you, let him be your servant;

* Matt. xx. 17-19. Mark x. 32-34. Luke xviii. 31-34.

even as the Son of Man came not to be served, but to serve, and to give his life a ransom for many." *

And he came to Jericho with his disciples, a great number of people following him; and two blind men were sitting by the wayside begging. And one of them, — Bartimeus, the son of Timeus, — hearing that it was Jesus of Nazareth who was passing by, began to cry out, and to say, "Jesus, thou Son of David, have mercy on me." And the multitude rebuked him, charging him to hold his peace. But he cried out the more, "Jesus, thou Son of David, have mercy on me." Then Jesus stood still, and directed them to be brought to him; and they called the blind *men*, saying, "Be of good comfort, rise, he calls for you." And Bartimeus casting away his garment rose, *and with the other blind man*, ran to Jesus; and Jesus said to them, "What would you, that I should do for you?" The blind men said to him, "Lord, open our eyes." Then Jesus touched their eyes, and said, "Go your way; your faith has made you whole." And immediately they received their sight, and followed Jesus in the

Two Blind Men. — Matthew and Mark speak of this miracle as taking place when Jesus was departing from Jericho, Luke of it when he had "come nigh" to it. Commentators have attempted to explain the discrepancy in various ways; but it seems incapable of explanation. The most natural supposition is that Luke, who was not an eye-witness, made an error of fact. The discrepancy proves conclusively that neither of the first three evangelists saw the accounts that were written by the others, and their narratives should, therefore, have all the more weight.

* Matt. xx. 20-28. Mark x. 35-45.

way, glorifying God. And when they saw it, all the people gave praise to God.*

Jesus entered and passed through Jericho; and there was a man there, named Zaccheus, who was the chief tax-gatherer, and a rich man. He was desirous of seeing what sort of a person Jesus was, but he could not on account of the crowd; for he was of low stature. And running on before, he climbed up a Sycamore tree to see him; for Jesus was to pass that way. When Jesus came to the place, he looked up, and seeing him, said to him, "Zaccheus, make haste, and come down, for to-day I must abide in your house." He made haste, and came down, and and received him joyfully. And all who saw it murmured, saying, "He is going to be the guest of a sinner." But Zaccheus stood up, and said to the Lord, "Lo! Lord, the half of my goods I give to the poor, and if I have taken anything from any man by false accusation, I restore him four-fold." And Jesus said to him, "This day has salvation come to this house, for he too, is a son of Abraham; and the Son of Man came to seek and to save the lost."

While they were listening to this he went on to speak a parable, because he was near Jerusalem, and they thought the kingdom of God would at once appear. "A certain nobleman," he said, "went to a far country to receive a kingdom, and then to return. And calling his ten servants, he gave them each an equal sum of money, and said to them, 'Employ this till I return.' But his countrymen hated him, and sent an embassy after him, to say, 'We would not have this

Matt. xx. 29-34. Mark x. 46-52. Luke xxiii. 35-43; xix. 1.

man to reign over us.' And on his return, after having received the kingdom, he directed those servants to whom he had given the money to be called to him; to know how much each man had gained by trading. Then the first came, and said, 'Lord, your pound has gained ten pounds.' And said he to him, 'Well done, good servant; because you have been faithful in a very small matter, be governor over ten cities.' And the second came to him, saying, 'Lord, your pound has gained five pounds.' And he said to him, 'Be you governor also over five cities.' And another came, and said, Lord, "Here is your pound; I have kept it laid up in a napkin, for I feared you; because you are a hard man, taking up what you did not lay down, and reaping where you did not sow.' His master said to him, 'Out of your own mouth will I condemn you, you wicked servant. You knew that I was a hard man, taking up what I did not lay down, and reaping what I did not sow. Why, then, gave you not my money to the exchangers, so, at my coming, I might have received it with interest.' And he said to his attendants, 'Take from him the pound, and give it to him that has ten pounds.' They said to him, 'Lord, he has ten times as much already.' But, I say to you, 'That to every one who has, more will be given; but from him who has not, even what he has will be taken away. But as for those mine enemies, who would not that I should reign over them, bring them here, and slay them before me." *

When he had thus spoken, he went on toward Jerusalem. And the Passover of the Jews was at hand,

* Luke xix. 2-27.

and many had gone up to Jerusalem from the country, to purify themselves before the Passover. And the Jews were looking for Jesus, and said one to another, as they were standing in the temple, "Think you he will not come to the festival?" Now, both the chief priests and the Pharisees, had given orders that if any man knew where he was, he should give information, that they might apprehend him. Then Jesus, six days before the passover, came to Bethany, where Lazarus was, whom he had raised from the dead. And a great many of the Jews, knowing that he was there, came, not merely on account of Jesus, but to see Lazarus, whom he had raised from the dead. But the chief priests proposed to put Lazarus to death also, because many of the Jews on his account drew off from them, and believed in Jesus.*

* Luke xix. 2-28. John x. 55-57; xii. 1, 9, 11.

PART SEVENTH.

THE PUBLIC ENTRY OF JESUS INTO JERUSALEM, AND SUBSEQUENT TRANSACTIONS.

TIME — FOUR DAYS.

LIFE OF JESUS.

PART SEVENTH.

NOW, the Jews who were with Jesus when he called Lazarus from the grave, had borne testimony that he raised him from the dead; and, for this reason, the great multitude who had come to the festival, when they heard, the next day, that Jesus was coming to Jerusalem, took branches of Palm trees, and went out to meet him.

And when Jesus was near Jerusalem, at Bethphage and Bethany on the Mount of Olives, he sent two of his disciples, saying: "Go to the village over against

Bethphage and Bethany.—Bethany was a small village on the eastern slope of the Mount of Olives; and Bethphage—which signifies the "place of figs,"—is supposed to have been a plantation on the mountain devoted to the cultivation of figs. Bethany was located about a mile from the summit of the mountain, and not far from where the road to Jericho makes an abrupt descent towards the valley of the Jordan. It is now a ruinous hamlet of about twenty houses, and in it are shown the traditional sites of the house of Simon the leper, and of the house and tomb of Lazarus.

The Mount of Olives, is separated from Jerusalem by the valley of the Kidron, which is dry in the hot season, but the bed of a small stream in winter. It is about a mile from the

you, and on entering, you will find an ass tied, and a colt with her, on which man never sat; loose them, and bring them to me. And if any one should say to you, 'Why are you doing this?' tell him that the Master has need of them, and he will send them directly." They went and found the ass and colt, tied at a door in the open street, at a place where two ways met, and they loosed them. And as they were loosing the colt, the owner, and others standing by, said: "Why are you loosing them?" They answered as Jesus had directed, "The Master has need of them;" and they let them go. Then they brought the ass and colt to Jesus, and putting their cloaks upon the colt, sat Jesus thereon.

All this was done to fulfil what had been written by the prophet, "Tell ye the daughter of Zion, Lo! thy king cometh to thee, meek and sitting upon an ass, and a colt the foal of an ass."

As he went a very great multitude spread their garments in the way; others cut down branches from the trees, and strewed them in the way; and when they came near the city, — at the foot of the Mount of Olives, — all of his disciples, and the multitude, rejoicing, began to praise God with loud voices, for all

city, and its summit affords a full view of Jerusalem and its environs. There are two roads from Bethany to Jerusalem, one around the southern slope of the mountain; the other — shorter but more difficult — over its summit. This latter is supposed to have been the one now taken by Jesus.

Spread their garments in the way. — The custom of spreading garments and flowers in the way of the great has always existed in the East. With this honor Agrippa was receïved when he came to Jerusalem.

the miracles that they had seen; and those that went before, and those that followed, cried, "Hosannah to the Son of David: Blessed is he that cometh in the name of the Lord: Blessed be the King that cometh in the name of the Lord: Peace in heaven and glory in the highest."

These things his disciples did not understand at the time, but after Jesus was glorified they remembered that they had been written concerning him, and had been done in regard to him.

Then the Pharisees said to one another, "You see that we effect nothing. Lo! the whole world is going after him." And some of them from among the multitude said to him, "Teacher, rebuke your disciples." He answered them: "I tell you, if they were to hold their peace, the very stones would cry out."

As he came near, he looked on the city, and wept over it, saying: "If thou hadst known, even at this thy time, what belongs to thy peace! but now it is hidden from thine eyes! For the day will come when thine enemies will cast a trench about thee, and shut thee in on every side, and lay thee even with the ground, and thy children within thee, not leaving in thee one stone upon another; because thou knewest not the time of thy visitation."

And on his entry into Jerusalem the whole city was

Hosannah is a Syriac word meaning "save I beseech thee." It here seems equivalent to, "Redress our grievances, and save us from our oppressors;" and its use by the multitude shows they believed that Jesus had then come to take possession of the (temporal) Messianic kingdom.

moved, asking: "Who is he?" The multitudes answered: "It is Jesus, the prophet of Nazareth in Galilee." And he went into the temple; and the blind, and the lame came to him there, and he healed them. But when the chief priests, and the teachers of the Law, saw the wonders which he did, and heard the children shouting in the temple, "Hosannah to the Son of David," they were angry and troubled, and said to him: "Hear you what these children are saying?" Jesus said to them: "Have you never read that from the mouth of babes and sucklings there is uttered praise?" When the evening had come he went out of the city to Bethany, and lodged there with the twelve.*

And on the morning of the morrow, as he returned to the city from Bethany, he was hungry. And, seeing a fig-tree at a distance in the road, he went to see if he could find fruit upon it; but when he came to it he found nothing but leaves, for the season of figs had not come. Then he said, "Let no one eat fruit from thee hereafter, forever." And his disciples heard this.

And Jesus went into the temple, and drove out those who sold and bought, and overturned the tables of the money-changers, and the seats of those who sold doves, and suffered no one to carry anything through the temple. And he said to them, "It is written, 'My house shall be a house of prayer for all nations;' but you have made it a den of thieves." The chief priests and the teachers of the Law heard what he said, and

*John xii. 12-19. Matt. xxi. 1-11, 14-17. Mark xi. 1-11. Luke xix. 29-44.

sought to destroy him ; for they feared him, because all the people were carried away by his teachings. But in the day time he taught in the temple, and in the evening he went out of the city, and abode in the Mount of Olives.*

In the morning, as they were passing by, they saw the fig-tree dried up from the roots. And Peter remembered, and said to Jesus, "Rabbi, see! the tree which you cursed has withered away." Jesus answered, "Have faith in God; for I tell you in truth that if you have faith and doubt not, you shall not only do what has been done to this fig-tree, but you shall say to this mountain, 'Be thou taken up, and cast into the sea,' and it shall be done. All things whatever that you may ask in prayer, believing, shall be given you."

They entered Jerusalem again, and as he was walking in the temple, the chief priests, and elders of the people came to him, and said, "By what authority are you acting thus? And who gave you the authority?" Jesus answered them, "I will also ask you a question; and if you answer me, I will tell you by what authority I act thus. Whence had John authority to baptize? From Heaven, or from men?" And they reasoned thus with themselves, "If we say, from Heaven, he will say, 'Why then did you not believe him;' but if we say, 'From men, there is danger from the multitude, for they all regard John as a prophet.' So, they answered Jesus, "We do not know." And he said to them, "Neither do I tell you by what authority I act thus."

* Matt. xi. 12, 13, 18. Mark xi. 12-19. Luke xix. 45-48; xxi. 37.

"But what think you? A certain man had two sons, and coming to the first, he said: 'Son, go, work to-day in my vineyard.' And he answered, 'I will not.' Afterward, however, he repented and went. And the man came to the other, and said to him the same; and he answered, 'I will, sir;' and went not. Which of the two did the will of his father?" They said: "The first." Jesus said to them, "I tell you in truth that the tax-gatherers and harlots are entering the kingdom of God before you; for John came to you preaching righteousness, and you did not hear him; but the tax-gatherers and harlots did; and yet when you saw that, you did not repent and listen to him." *

"Hear another parable: A certain householder planted a vineyard, put a hedge about it, dug a winevat in it, and built a watch-tower; and then, letting it out to husbandmen, went for a long time to a distant country. And when the season for fruit drew near, he sent to the husbandmen a servant to receive of the fruit of the vineyard. But they seized him, beat him, and sent him away empty. Then he sent to them another servant; and they cast stones at him, wounded him, and sent him away shamefully handled. Then he sent again another, and him they killed; and then others, many in number, and they treated them in the same manner, — beating some and killing others. Then the master of the vineyard said, "What shall I do? I have one son, my well-beloved, I will

Receive of the fruit. — It was the ancient custom to pay rent in the produce of a farm or vineyard.

* Matt. xxi. 23-32. Mark xi. 23-32. Luke xx. 1-8.

send him. It may be they will respect my son.' But the husbandmen said among themselves, 'This is the heir. Come, let us kill him, and seize upon the inheritance.' And they laid hold of him, thrust him out of the vineyard, and killed him.

"What, then, will the owner of the vineyard do to those husbandmen? He will come and destroy them, and give the vineyard to others who will render to him its produce in the proper season." And some that heard this said, "God forbid." But, looking on them, Jesus said, "What, then, is this that is written: 'The stone which the builders rejected has become the head of the corner. This is the Lord's doing, and it is wonderful in our eyes.' Therefore, I say to you, the kingdom will be taken from you, and given to a nation bringing forth its fruits; and whoever stumbles against this stone, will be sorely bruised; but on whom it falls, it will grind him to powder."

The chief priests and Pharisees, when they heard these parables, perceived that he was speaking against them, and they wished to lay hands on him, — but did not, for fear of the multitude, who regarded him as a prophet.*

Jesus spoke to them again in parables, saying: "The kingdom of heaven is like a certain king, who made a marriage feast for his son; and sent his ser-

On whom it falls it will grind him to powder. — When a criminal was stoned among the Jews, he was thrown from a scaffolding some fifteen feet high, upon a heap of stones. If he was not killed by the fall, a heavy stone was thrown upon him, and it "ground him to powder."

* Matt. xxi. 33-46. Mark xii. 1-12. Luke xx. 9-19.

vants to call those that were bidden to the wedding; and they would not come. Then he sent other servants, saying: Tell them which are bidden, 'Behold, I have prepared my dinner, my oxen and my fatlings are killed, and all things are ready; come to the marriage.' But some of them made light of it, and went off, one to his farm, another to his merchandise; and the remnant took his servants, and treated them spitefully, and slew them. But when the king heard of it, he was enraged, and sent his armies, and destroyed those murderers, and burned their city. Then he said to his servants, 'The feast is ready, but those bidden were not worthy. Go, therefore, into the highways, and whoever you find, ask to the marriage.' So the servants went out into the highways, and collected all, as many as they found, bad and good; and the wedding was furnished with guests. But when the king came in to see the guests, he saw a man there who had not on a wedding garment. He said to him, 'Friend, how came you in here, not having on a wedding garment?' And he was struck dumb. Then said the king to the servants, 'Bind him hand and foot, and cast him into the outer darkness; where will be weeping and gnashing of teeth.' For many are called, but few are chosen." *

Then the Pharisees went away and plotted how they might entangle him with questions. And they sent to him certain of their disciples, and of the Herodians to

The Herodians.—A political party formed, no doubt, by Herod the Great. They held that it was lawful to render tribute to Cæsar, and also right to adopt the religious rites

Matt. xxii. 1-14.

watch him, and, feigning themselves righteous men, to take hold of his words, so that they might deliver him to the power of the governor. And when they had come to him, they said: "Master, we know that you are a just man, and teach the way of God in truth, not fearing any; for you regard not the rank of a man. Tell us then, what think you? Is it lawful to pay tribute to Cesar, or not? Shall we pay it, or shall we not pay it?" But Jesus perceiving their wickedness, said: "Why do you thus question me, hypocrites? Show me the tribute money?" They brought him a denarius; and he said to them, "Whose is this image and inscription?" They answered, "Cesar's." He said to them, "Render, then, to Cesar what is Cesar's, and to God what is God's." And hearing this they were confounded, and went away, seeing that they could not take hold of his words before the people.*

The same day certain of the Sadducees (who deny that there is any resurrection) came to him, and questioned him, saying: "Master, Moses wrote that if a man die, having no children, his brother shall marry his wife, and raise up heirs to his brother. Now there were seven brothers, and the first took a wife, and dying, left no child. And the second took her, and left no child, and the third likewise; and in like manner the seven also, and they all died, leaving no children; last of all the woman died also. In the resurrection,

and customs of their conquerors. The Pharisees held opposite opinions, therefore Jesus was in danger of being entangled if his answer favored the one or the other party.

*Matt. xxii. 15-22. Mark xii. 13-17. Luke xx. 20-26.

whose wife will she be of the seven? for they all had her." Jesus answered them, "You err, not knowing the Scriptures, nor the power of God. The children of this world marry, and are given in marriage; but those who are accounted worthy to obtain that world, and the resurrection from the dead, neither marry, nor are given in marriage. Neither do they die any more; for they are equal to the angels, and are the children of God, being the children of the resurrection. And touching the resurrection of the dead; have you not read what was spoken by God in the book of Moses? How in the bush he said, 'I am the God of Abraham, and the God of Isaac, and the God of Jacob?' He is not the God of the dead, but the God of the living; for all live to him. You, therefore, greatly err." And the multitude who heard this, were greatly moved by his teaching, and certain of the Scribes said, "Master, thou hast well said." *

The Pharisees, hearing that he had put the Sadducees to silence, gathered about him, and one of them —a teacher of the Law,—perceiving that he had answered them well, asked, to try him, "Which is the greatest commandment of all?" Jesus answered, "The first of all the commandments is, 'Hear, O Israel; the Lord our God is the only Lord; and thou shalt love the Lord thy God, with all thy heart, and with all thy soul, and with all thy mind, and with all thy strength.' This is the first commandment. And the second is like it, 'Thou shalt love thy neighbor as thyself.' There are no commandments greater than these; and on these two hang all the law and the prophets."

*Matt. xxii. 23-33. Mark xii. 18-27. Luke xx. 27-40.

And the teacher of the Law said to him, "Well, Master, thou hast said the truth; for there is one God; and there is no other besides him; and to love him with all the heart, and all the understanding, and all the soul, and all the strength; and to love one's neighbor as one's self, is more than all burnt offerings and sacrifices." Then Jesus, seeing that he had answered wisely, said to him, "You are not far from the kingdom of God." *

While the Pharisees were gathered about him in the temple, Jesus asked them, "What think you of Christ? Whose son is he?" They said to him, "The son of David." He said to them, "How, then, does David, by the Holy Spirit in the Psalms, call him Lord, saying, 'The Lord said to my Lord, Sit thou on my right hand, till I make thine enemies thy footstool?' If David call him Lord, how then is he David's son?" No one was able to answer him a word, neither durst any one, from that day forth, ask him any more questions.†

But the common people heard him gladly, and he said to them and to his disciples, "The teachers of the Law and the Pharisees, sit in the seat of Moses. All, therefore, that they bid you, observe and do; but do not according to their works; for they say, and do not. They bind up heavy burdens, and hard to be borne, and lay them on men's shoulders; but will not themselves move them with a finger. And all their works they do to be seen by men. They wear broad phylacteries, and wide fringes on their garments; and

* Matt. xxii. 34-40. Mark xii. 28-34.

† Matt. xxii. 41-46. Mark xii. 35-37. Luke xx. 41-44.

love first places at feasts, and the highest seats in the synagogues, and greetings in the market-places, and to go in long robes, and to be called of men, 'Rabbi, Rabbi.' But, be not you called Rabbi; for you have only one Master, even Christ; and you are all brothers. And call no man your father on the earth; for one is your Father, who is in heaven. Nor be you called leaders, for you have only one leader, even Christ. But let the greatest among you be your servant; for whoever shall exalt himself will be humbled; and he that shall humble himself will be exalted.*

"But woe for you, Scribes and Pharisees, hypocrites! for you shut the kingdom of heaven against men, not going in yourselves, nor suffering those that are entering to go in. Woe for you, Scribes and Pharisees, hypocrites! for you devour widows' houses, and for a pretence, make long prayers; therefore you will receive the greater damnation. Woe for you, Scribes and Pharisees, hypocrites! for you compass sea and land to make one proselyte; and when he is made, you make him twofold more a child of hell than yourselves. Woe for you, blind guides, who say, 'If any one swear by the temple, it is nothing; but if he swear by the gold of the temple, he is bound by his oath.' Fools and blind! Which is greater, the gold, or the temple that sanctifies the gold? And, 'If any one swear by the altar, it is nothing; but if he swear by the gift that is upon it, he is bound.' Fools and blind! Which is greater, the gift, or the altar that sanctifies the gift? He who swears by the altar, swears by it, and by all that is upon it. And he who

* Mark xii. 38-39. Luke xx. 45, 46. Matt. xxiii. 1-12.

swears by the temple, swears by it, and by Him who dwells within it. And he who swears by heaven, swears by the throne of God, and by Him who sits upon it. Woe for you, Scribes and Pharisees, hypocrites! for you pay tithes of mint, and anise, and cummin, and neglect the weightier matters of the Law, judgment, mercy, and truth. These ought you to have done, and not to have left the other undone. You blind guides! you strain out a gnat, and swallow a camel. Woe for you, Scribes and Pharisees, hypocrites! for you make clean your cups and dishes, but are full of extortion and excess. Thou blind Pharisee! cleanse first that which is within the cup and platter, that the outside may be clean also. Woe for you, Scribes and Pharisees, hypocrites! for you are like whited sepulchres, which indeed appear beautiful outwardly, but are within full of dead men's bones, and all uncleanness. So, you also outwardly appear righteous to men, but are within full of hypocrisy and iniquity. Woe for you, Scribes and Pharisees, hypocrites! for you build the tombs of the prophets, and garnish the sepulchres of the righteous, and say, 'If we had lived in the days of our fathers, we would not have been partakers with them in the blood of the prophets;' whereby you bear testimony against yourselves, that you are the children of those who killed

Strain out a gnat. — In Eastern countries gnats swarm about the wine vats, and fill the wine vessels. Therefore the wine is strained before drinking.

Whited Sepulchres. — The tombs were whitened every year to render them conspicious, so that strangers who came to the festivals, might not become unclean by inadvertently coming in contact with them.

the prophets. Fill you up, then, the measure of your fathers. Serpents! Brood of vipers! how can you escape the damnation of hell? Lo! I shall send to you prophets, and wise men, and teachers; and some of them you will kill and crucify, and some you will scourge in your synagogues, and persecute from city to city; so that upon you shall come all the righteous blood shed in the land, from the blood of righteous Abel to the blood of Zechariah, son of Barachias, whom you slew between the temple and the altar. Truly, I say to you, all this will come upon this generation. O Jerusalem, Jerusalem! Thou that killest the prophets, and stonest those that are sent to thee; how often would I have gathered thy children together, even as a hen gathers her chickens under her wings, and you would not! Lo! your house is left to you desolate. For I say to you, you shall not see me henceforth, till you shall say, 'Blessed is he that cometh in the name of the Lord." *

And looking up, Jesus saw some rich men casting their gifts into the treasury; and with them he saw a poor widow casting in two mites, which make a farthing. And calling to him his disciples, he said to them, "Of a truth I tell you, this poor widow has cast in more than they all. For they all have given from their abundance; but she, from her penury, has cast in all that she had, even all her living." *

Among those that came up to worship at the festival, were certain Greeks, and they came to Philip, who was of Bethsaida of Galilee, and made request of him,

* Matt. xxiii. 13-39. Mark xii. 40. Luke xx. 47.
† Mark xii. 41-44. Luke xxi. 1-4.

saying, "Sir, we wish to see Jesus." Philip went and told Andrew; and then Andrew and Philip told Jesus. Jesus answered them, "The hour has come for the Son of Man to be glorified. Truly, truly, I tell you, unless a grain of wheat fall into the ground and die, it remains alone; but if it die, it brings forth many grains. He who loves his life will lose it; and he who hates his life in this world, will keep it to life eternal. If any one would serve me, let him follow me; and where I am, there also will my servant be; If any one serve me, him will my Father honor.

"Now is my soul troubled; and what shall I say? Father! save me from this hour? Nay; it was for this I came, — for this hour. Father! glorify thy name."

Then there came a voice from heaven, saying, "I have glorified it, and will glorify it again." The people who stood by and heard, said that it thundered; others said, "An angel has spoken to him." Jesus said, "This voice came not for my sake, but for yours.

"Now is the judgment of this world: now will the ruler of this world be cast out, and I, when I shall be lifted up from the earth, shall draw all men to me." This he said, signifying what kind of death he was to die. The people answered him, "We have heard out of the Law that the Christ is to remain forever; how then say you that the Son of Man shall be lifted up? Who is this Son of Man?" Then Jesus said to them, "Yet a little while is the light with you. Walk while you have the light, lest the darkness overtake you; for he that walks in darkness knows not where he

To remain forever. — The common notion among the Jews was that the Messianic kingdom was to last a thousand years.

goes. While you have the light, believe in the light, that you may be the children of light." Thus spoke Jesus, and departed, hiding himself from them.*

But though he had done so many miracles before them, they did not believe in him. And thus was fulfilled what was said by the prophet Isaiah. "Lord, who hath believed our report; and to whom hath the arm of the Lord been revealed?" Hence they could not believe; for Isaiah says again: "He has blinded their eyes, and hardened their hearts, so that they do not see with their eyes, nor understand with their hearts, nor turn from their ways that I may heal them." Thus said Isaiah when he saw his glory, and spoke of him. Yet, indeed, many even of the rulers believed in him; but on account of the Pharisees they did not profess their belief, for fear of being put out of the synagogue. For they loved the praise of men more than the praise of God.

But Jesus had proclaimed, "He who believes in me, believes not in me, but in Him who sent me; and he who sees me sees him who sent me. I have come a light into the world, that no man who believes in me may remain in darkness. If any one hears my words and regards them not, I do not judge him; for I came not to judge, but to save the world. There is a judge for him who rejects me, and receives not my words; the truths I have taught, they will pass judgment on him at the last day. For I have not spoken from myself; but He who sent me, the Father himself, has commanded me what to say and what to teach; and I know that his word is life eternal.

*John xii. 20-36.

Whatever I teach, therefore, I teach as the Father has given me direction." *

As he went out of the temple one of his disciples said to him, "Master, see you what goodly stones and gifts, and buildings are here?" Jesus answered, "As for these things, the day will come when not one stone will be left on another, that will not be thrown down."

And as he was sitting on the Mount of Olives, over against the temple, Peter and James, and John, and Andrew, came to him privately, and said: "Tell us when this will be; and what will be the sign when all these things are coming to an end?" Jesus answered them, "See that no one deceive you; for many will come in my name, saying, 'I am Christ,' and will deceive many; and you will hear of wars and rumors of wars; but be not disturbed, for all this must be; but the end is not yet. For nation will rise against nation, and kingdom against kingdom; and there will be famines, and pestilences, and commotions in many places. These will be the beginning of sorrows. But look to yourselves; for they will deliver you over to the courts of law, and you will be scourged in the synagogues, and brought before governors and kings

Not one stone will be left on another.—This prediction was literally fulfilled. The temple was dug up from its foundations, and the ploughshare passed over its site.

Saying "I am Christ."—So many of these impostors appeared in the time of Nero, when Felix was procurator of Judea, that numbers are said to have been seized and executed every year.

*John xii. 37-50.

for my sake; for a testimony to them. And the glad tidings must first be proclaimed to all nations. But when they deliver you over as criminals, be not anxious what you shall say, nor prepare yourselves beforehand; but whatever may be given you at the time, speak, for it will not be you who will speak, but the Holy Spirit. Settle it therefore in your hearts not to deliberate what to say; for I will give you a speech and wisdom which none of your adversaries will be able to gainsay or resist. Brother will deliver up brother to death, and the father his child, and children will rise against their parents, and cause them to be put to death. And you will be hated by all men for my sake; but he who endures to the end will be saved. And this glad news of the kingdom will be preached in all the world for a testimony to all nations, and then will the end come. By your patience preserve your souls. When, therefore, you shall see Jerusalem encompassed with armies, and the desolating abomination spoken of by Daniel the prophet standing upon holy ground, — let whoever reads understand, — then let those who are in Judea flee to the mountains; and let not those that are in the country enter therein; let not him who is on the housetop go down to take anything out of his house; nor let him that is in the field turn back to take up his garment. For these are the days of vengeance, when all things that are written will be fulfilled. But woe for such as are with child, and for such as are marrying, in those days! and pray that your flight may not be in winter, nor on a Sab-

The desolating abomination. — The Roman armies with their idolatrous standards, encamped on holy ground.

bath day; for there will be great distress in the land, and affliction on this people — such as has not been since the beginning of the world, no, nor ever will be. They will fall by the edge of the sword, and be led away captive to all nations; and Jerusalem will be trodden down by the Gentiles, till the times of the Gentiles are ended; and were not those days to be shortened, all would perish; but for the sake of the chosen, those days will be shortened. Then, should any one say to you, 'Lo! here is Christ,' or 'He is there,' believe him not; for false Christs and false teachers will rise up, showing great signs and wonders so as to deceive, if it were possible, the very chosen. Lo! I have told you beforehand: should they say to you, 'Lo! he is in the desert;' go not forth. 'Lo! he is in some private chamber;' believe it not. For the coming of the Son of Man will be like the lightning which flashes from the east to the west. But where the carcass is, there the eagles will gather together.

"Then, immediately after the affliction of those days, the sun will be darkened; and the moon will not give her light; and the stars will fall from heaven, and the host of heaven will be shaken! And upon the earth will be distress of nations and perplexity; men's hearts failing them for fear, and for looking for those things that are coming on the land. And then the sign of the Son of Man will appear in heaven; and all the tribes of the land will mourn when they

Nor on the Sabbath. — A Jew was allowed to journey only two thousand cubits — about three-fourths of a mile — on the Sabbath.

shall see the Son of Man coming in the clouds with power and great glory. When these things begin to take place, look up, and lift up your heads, for your deliverance is at hand; for then shall the Son of Man send forth his angels with a loud sound of trumpets, to gather together his chosen from the four winds, from one end of heaven to the other.

"Now learn a lesson from the fig-tree: when its branches are tender, and it puts forth leaves, you know that summer is near. So, when you see these things coming to pass, know that the end is nigh, even at the door. Truly, I say to you, this generation will not pass away, till all these things be done. Heaven and earth may pass away, but my words cannot pass away. But of the day and the hour knows no man; no, not the angels of heaven, not the Son, but my Father only. Look to yourselves, therefore, lest at any time your hearts should be overcharged with surfeiting and drunkenness, and the cares of this life, and so that day should come upon you unawares; for as a snare will it come on all that dwell on the face of the whole land. As when a traveller leaves his house, and gives charge of it to his servants, and appoints to each his work, and charges the housekeeper to watch, so do you watch; for you know not when the master of the house will come, whether at evening, or at midnight, or at the cock-crowing, or in the morning. Let him not come suddenly, and find you sleeping. And what I say to you, I say to all; Watch! Watch and pray, that you may be thought worthy to escape all these things, and to stand before the Son of Man.

"Then the kingdom of heaven will be like ten

virgins, who took their lamps, and went forth to meet the bridegroom. And five of them were wise, and five were foolish. The foolish took lamps, but took no oil with them; but the wise took oil in their vessels with their lamps. And as the bridegroom was long in coming, they all grew drowsy and fell asleep. But at midnight there was a cry, 'Lo! the bridegroom is coming, go forth to meet him.' Then all those virgins arose, and trimmed their lamps. And the foolish said to the wise, 'Give us of your oil; for our lamps are going out.' But the wise answered, 'Not so; lest there be not enough for us and you; go you rather to those that sell and buy for yourselves.' But while they were gone to buy, the bridegroom came, and those who were ready, went in with him to the feast, and the door was shut. Afterward came the other virgins, and said: 'Lord, Lord, open to us.' But he answered, 'Truly, I say to you, I know you not.' Watch, therefore, for you know neither the day nor the hour when the Son of Man comes. It will be as when a man going to a distant country called his servants, and delivered to them his property; giving to one five talents, to another two, and to another one; to each according to his ability; and setting out at once on his journey. Then he who had received the five talents, went and traded with them, and made other five talents. And also he who had received two, he gained other two. But he who had received the one talent, went and dug in the earth, and hid his lord's money. After a long time the lord of those servants came, and had a reckoning with them. And he who had received the five talents, came and brought other five talents, saying, 'Lord, you gave me five talents, see I have gained beside them five talents more.' His lord said to him, 'Well done, good and faithful servant; you have been faithful over a few things, I will give you charge over many things; enter into the joy of thy lord.' He also who had received the two talents came, and said, 'Lord, you gave me two talents; see, I have gained besides them two other talents.' His lord said to him, 'Well done, good and faithful servant; you have been faithful over a few things, I will give you charge over many things; enter into the joy of thy lord.' Then he who had received the one talent came, and said, 'Lord, I knew you were a hard man, reaping where you had not sown, and gathering where you had not strewed; and I was afraid, and went and hid your talent in the ground; see, you have your own again.' But his lord answered, 'Bad and slothful servant, you knew that I reap where I have not sowed, and gather where I have not strewed: you ought then to have put my money with the exchangers, that at my coming I might receive my own with interest. Take, therefore, the talent from this man, and give it to him who has the ten talents. For to every one who has will be given, and he shall have abundance; but from him who has not, will be taken away even what he has. And cast the unprofitable servant into outer darkness; where will be weeping and gnashing of teeth.'

"When the Son of Man comes in his glory, and all the holy angels with him, he will sit on the throne of his glory; and before him will be gathered all nations; and he will separate them one from another, as a shepherd separates his sheep from the goats; and he will set the sheep on his right hand, but the goats on the left. Then will the King say to those on his right hand, 'Come, ye blessed of my Father, inherit the kingdom prepared for you from the foundation of the world: For I was hungry, and you gave me food: I was thirsty, and you gave me drink: I was a stranger, and you took me in: naked, and you clothed me: I was sick, and you visited me: I was in prison, and you came to me." Then will the righteous answer him, 'Lord, when saw we you hungry, and gave you food, or thirsty, and gave you drink? When saw we you a stranger, and took you in? or naked, and clothed you? Or when saw we you sick, or in prison, and came to you?' And the King will say, 'Truly, I say to you, in that you have done it to one of the least of these my brethren you have done it to me.' Then will he say to them on the left hand, 'Depart from me, ye cursed, into everlasting fire, prepared for the devil and his angels: for I was hungry, and you gave me no food; thirsty, and you gave me no drink; I was a stranger, and you took me not in; naked, and you clothed me not; sick, and in prison, and you visited me not.' Then will they also answer, 'Lord, when saw we you hungry, or athirst, or a stranger, or naked, or sick, or in prison, and did not minister to you?" Then will he answer them, "Truly, I say to you, in that you did it not to one of the least of these, you did it not to me.' And these will go away into everlasting punishment; but the righteous into life eternal." *

* Matt. xxiv. 1-51; xxv. 1-46. Mark xiii. 1-37. Luke xxi. 5-36.

When Jesus had finished all these sayings, he said to his disciples, "You know that after two days is the festival of the passover, and that the Son of Man will be betrayed to be crucified."

Then the chief priests the Scribes, and the elders of the people, assembled in the palace of the high priest, whose name was Caiaphas, and consulted how they might take Jesus by subtlety, and kill him. But, they said, "Not on the feast-days, lest there be an uproar among the people."

And Jesus being in Bethany, in the house of Simon the leper, they made him a supper, and Martha served; but Lazarus was one of those who were at table with him. Then Mary took an alabaster box — very costly — and broke the box, and poured the ointment on his head as he reclined at table; and she also anointed the feet of Jesus, and wiped them with her hair; and the house was filled with the odor of the ointment. But when his disciples saw this they were indignant, and murmured against Mary; and one of them — Judas, son of Simon Iscariot, who was to betray him — said: "To what purpose was this waste? Why was not this ointment sold for three hundred denarii, and given to the poor?" This he said not that he cared for the poor; but because he was a thief, and bore the purse of the disciples. When Jesus understood it, he said to them: "Why trouble you the woman? Let her alone. The poor you have always with you, but me you have not always. She has done a good work on me. She has come beforehand to anoint my body for my burial. Truly, I tell you, wherever my Gospel shall be preached throughout the whole world, this that she has done, will be told as a memorial of her."

Then Satan entered into Judas, called Iscariot, and he went away to the chief priests and captains, and said to them, "What will you give me, if I deliver him to you?" And, when they heard this, they were glad, and agreed to give him thirty pieces of silver. And he promised and sought opportunity to betray him to them in the absence of the multitude.

Now on the first day of the feast of unleavened bread, when the passover is killed, the disciples came to Jesus, saying, "Where wilt thou that we prepare to eat the passover?" And he sent Peter and John, saying to them: "Go you into the city, and there will meet you a man bearing a pitcher of water; follow him, and wherever he shall go in, say you to the good man of the house, 'The Master says my time is at hand; where is the guest-chamber? for I will eat the passover at thy house with my disciples.' He will show you a large upper room furnished and prepared; there make ready for us." His disciples went into the city, and found as he had said to them; and they made ready the passover.

PART EIGHTH.

THE LAST SUPPER, AND THE CRUCIFIXION.

TIME — TWO DAYS.

LIFE OF JESUS.

PART EIGHTH.

WHEN the evening had come he placed himself at table with the twelve apostles, and said to them: "I have earnestly desired to eat this Passover with you before I suffer; for, I tell you, I shall not eat of it again until it be accomplished in the kingdom of God." And taking a cup he gave thanks, and said, "Take this, and divide it among you; for I tell you, I shall not again drink of the fruit of the vine, until the kingdom of God has come."

There existed a rivalry among them as to which was the greatest. But he said to them, "The kings of the Gentiles exercise lordship over them, and those having authority over them, they call Benefactors; but it must not be so with you. Let the greatest among you be as the youngest, and the chief, as he who serves. For which is greater, he who reclines at tables, or he who serves? Is not he who is at table?

There existed a rivalry among them.—This rivalry was often manifested previously. It seems now to have shown itself in a contention for the first places at table. Notwithstanding their Master's frequent predictions of his death, the disciples were still in expectation of his founding a temporal kingdom.

But I am among you as as one who serves. You have continued with me in my trials, and I appoint to you a kingdom, as my Father has appointed one to me; that you may eat and drink at my table in my kingdom, and may sit on thrones, ruling the twelve tribes of Israel." *

Then Jesus, knowing that the Father had committed all things into his hands, and that he had come from God, and was going to God, rose from supper, and, laying aside his cloak, took a towel, and girded himself. After this he poured water into a basin, and began to wash the feet of the disciples, and to wipe them with the towel with which he was girded. But when he came to Simon Peter, Peter said to him: "Lord, do you wash my feet?" Jesus answered: "What I am doing you do not understand now; but you will know shortly." Peter said to him, "You shall never wash my feet." Jesus answered: "If I wash you not, you have nothing in common with me." Then Simon Peter said to him: "Lord, not my feet only, but my hands and my head." Jesus answered: "He who is washed needs to wash only his feet to be altogether clean; and you are clean, but not all." He knew who was about to betray him, therefore, he said, "You are not all clean." After he had washed their

Girded himself. — Servants, when waiting at table, laid aside their outer garments, and were girded with a towel.

Needs to wash only his feet. — As the Jews wore sandals, the feet required frequent washing; and if one had bathed wholly during the day, he was, with the washing of his feet, "altogether clean."

*Matt. xxvi. 20. Mark xiv. 17. Luke xxii. 14-18, 24-30.

feet, and taken his cloak, he placed himself again at table, and said to them: "Know now what I have done to you. You call me Master and Lord, and you say well, for so I am. If I, then, your Master and Lord, have washed your feet, you ought also to wash one another's feet. I have given you an example that you also may do as I have done for you. Truly, truly, I tell you, the servant is not greater than the Master, nor he that is sent greater than he that sends him. Knowing these things, happy will you be if you do them. I speak not of you all: I know whom I have chosen; but he I chose that the Scriptures may be fulfilled. 'He who eats of the loaf with me has lifted up his heel against me.' I tell you now before it comes to pass, that when it comes, you may believe that I am He. Truly, truly, I tell you, he who receives one that I send, receives me, and he who receives me, receives Him who sent me." *

While he was thus speaking, and they were eating, Jesus was troubled in spirit, and said to them: "Truly, truly, I say to you, One of you whose hand is with mine on the table, will betray me." Then the disciples looked one at another, doubting of whom he spoke; and they began to be sorrowful, and to say to him, one by one: "Lord, is it I? Is it I?" Jesus answered: "He who dips his hand with me in the dish, he it is who betrays me. The Son of Man indeed goes as it is written of him, but alas for that man by whom the Son of Man is betrayed! It had been better for him had he never been born."

Now one of the disciples whom Jesus loved, was leaning on his bosom, and Simon Peter made signs to

*John xiii. 3-20.

him to ask who it was of whom he spoke. He, leaning back on the breast of Jesus, said to him, "Lord, who is it?" Jesus answered, "He to whom I shall give the morsel, when I have dipped it." And, having dipped the morsel, he gave it to Judas Iscariot, the son of Simon. Judas said to him, "Master, is it I?" Jesus answered: "You have said." Then Satan entered into Judas, and Jesus said to him, "What you do, do quickly." (But no one at the table knew why he said this. Some thought that as Judas carried the purse, Jesus meant he should buy what was needed against the festival, or that he should give something to the poor.) Then, having received the morsel, Judas went out immediately, — and it was night.

When he had gone out, Jesus said, "Now is the Son of Man glorified, and God is glorified in him. And as God is glorified in him, so God will glorify him in himself, and will immediately glorify him. My children, but a little while shall I be with you. You will seek me, and, as I said to the Jews so now I say to you, where I go you cannot come. A new commandment I give to you, that you love one another, — that you love one another as I have loved you. By this will all men know that you are my disciples, if you have love one for another." *

Dipped it. — The sauce in which herbs and bread were dipped when eaten, was called *charoseth.* It was composed of dates, figs, almonds, apples, and other fruits, beaten together, and mixed with wine and aromatics, and strewed over with broken cinnamon, to represent the straw and clay used by the Israelites in making bricks in Egypt. BUXTORF.

* Matt. xxvi. 21-25. Mark xiv. 18-21. Luke xxii. 21-23. John xiii. 21-35.

Simon Peter said to him, "Lord, where do you go?" Jesus answered: "I go where you cannot follow now; but you will follow hereafter." Peter said to him: "Lord, why cannot I follow you now? I will lay down my life for you." Jesus answered, "Will you lay down your life for me? Truly, truly, I tell you, all of you will be offended with me this night; for it is written: 'I will smite the shepherd, and the sheep will be scattered.' But after I have risen, I will go before you to Galilee." Peter answered: "Though all should be offended with you, I will not be offended." Then the Master said: "Simon, Simon, Satan has desired you, to sift you like wheat; but I have prayed for you, that your strength may not fail; and when you return to me, strengthen your brethren." Peter said, "Lord, I am ready to lay down my life for you; to go with you to prison, or to death." Jesus answered: "Are you ready to lay down your life for me? Truly, truly, I say to you, the cock will not crow this night till you have thrice denied that you know me." But Peter said the more vehemently, "Though I should die with you, yet I will not deny you." And so said all the disciples.

Jesus said to them, "When I sent you without purse, or bag, or sandals, were you in want of anything?" They said to him: "Of nothing." Then he said to them, "But now, let him who has a purse take it, and a bag also; and let him who has no sword, sell his cloak and buy one; for that is yet to be fulfilled which

Let him sell his cloak and buy a sword. — "The language of this passage is highly figurative. Jesus reminds his disciples that formerly they might rely on the hospitality of their

is written, 'And he was reckoned among the malefactors.' And, indeed, my course is near an end." Then they said: "Lord lo! here are two swords." He answered, "Enough has been said." *

And as they were eating, Jesus took bread, and giving thanks, broke it, and gave it to them, saying: "Take, eat, this is my body which is broken for you: this do in remembrance of me." And in the same manner, after supper, he took the cup, and when he had given thanks, he gave it to them, saying: "Drink you all of this; for this is my blood of the new covenant which is shed for you, and for many, for the remission of sins; this do, as often as you drink it, in remembrance of me. But, I say to you, I will no more drink of the fruit of the vine, until the day when I drink it new with you in my Father's kingdom." †

"Let not your hearts be troubled; Have faith in God, and have faith also in me. In my Father's house are many mansions; if it were not so, I would have

countrymen; but now he had been rejected by the nation, and was about to be crucified with robbers; and they, his followers, must look for no favor. When the disciples produced the two swords, it is not to be supposed that they understood their Master literally. It was natural to do so, without any definite purpose. It is probable that they did not fully comprehend his meaning, and supposed that by showing the swords they might induce him to make a further explanation; but he was not disposed to do so." NORTON.

Many mansions. — The palaces of Eastern kings were very

* John xiii. 36-38. Matt. xxvi. 31-35. Mark xiv. 27-31, Luke xxii. 31-38.

† Matt. xxvi. 26-29. Mark xiv. 22-25. Luke xxii. 19, 20. 1 Cor. xi. 23-25.

told you. I go to prepare a place for you. And as I go to prepare a place for you, I will come again and receive you to myself, that where I am, you may be also. And where I go, you know, and the way you know."

Thomas said to him, "Lord, we know not where you go; and how can we know the way?"

Jesus said to him, "I am the way, and the truth, and the life; no man comes to the Father, but by me. Had you known me, you would have known my Father also; and now you know him, and have seen him."

Philip said to him, "Lord, show us the Father, and we shall be satisfied."

Jesus said to him, "Have I been so long with you, and have you not known me, Philip? He who has seen me, has seen the Father; and how say you, 'Show us the Father?' Believe you not that I am in the Father, and the Father in me? The words that I speak to you, I speak not of myself; and the Father, who dwells in me, he does the works. Believe me that I am in the Father, and the Father in me; if not, believe me for the very works' sake.

"Truly, truly, I say to you, he that believes in me, shall do the works that I do; and greater works than these shall he do; for I am going to my Father. And whatever you shall ask in my name, I will do, that the Father may be glorified in the Son. If you shall ask anything in my name, I will do it.

"If you love me keep my commandments; and I

extensive, and it was the custom of the monarchs to allow large numbers of their courtiers to dwell in them.

will ask the Father, and he will give you another Comforter, who will abide with you forever, — the Spirit of Truth, which the world cannot receive, because it sees him not, neither knows him; but you know him, for he dwells with you, and shall be in you.

"I will not leave you comfortless; I will come to you. A little while only, and the world will see me no more; but you will see me; and because I live, you shall live also.

"Then you will know that I am in my Father, and you in me, and I in you. He who keeps in mind my commandments, and does them, he it is that loves me; and he that loves me, will be loved of my Father, and I will love him, and will manifest myself to him."

Judas (not Iscariot) said to him, "Lord, how is it that you will manifest yourself to us, and not to the world?"

Jesus answered, "Whoever loves me, will keep my words; and my Father will love him, and we will come to him, and make our abode with him. He who loves me not, keeps not my words; and the words which you hear are not mine, but the Father's who sent me."

"These things have I spoken to you, while yet with you. But the Comforter, the Holy Spirit, whom the Father will send for my sake, he will teach you all things, and bring to your remembrance all that I have said to you.

"Peace I leave with you; my peace I give to you; not as the world gives peace give I to you. Let not your hearts be troubled, neither be afraid. You have heard how I said to you, I go away, and come again to you. If you loved me, you would rejoice, because I go to the Father; for the Father is greater than I. And now I tell you before it comes to pass, that, when it comes to pass, you may believe.

"I will no longer talk much with you; for the prince of this world comes, and with me he has nothing in common. But this must be that the world may know that I love the Father, and that as the Father has commanded me, so I do. Arise, let us go hence." *

"I am the true vine, and my Father is the husbandman. Every branch of mine that bears not fruit he cuts away; and every branch that bears fruit, he prunes, that it may bring forth more fruit. Now you are pruned through the words I have spoken to you. Abide in me, and I in you. As the branch cannot bear fruit unless it abides in the vine; so you cannot unless you abide in me. I am the vine, you are the branches. He that abides in me, and I in him, will bring forth much fruit; but severed from me you can do nothing. Whoever abides not in me, will be cast forth as a withered branch; and such, men gather and cast into the fire to be burned. If you abide in me, and my words abide in you, you shall ask whatever you will, and it will be granted you. Herein is my Father glorified, in your bearing much fruit; so shall you be my disciples.

"As the Father has loved me, so have I loved you;

Arise, let us go hence. — It is probable that Jesus rose and prayed, and then, before leaving the room, continued his discourse, and uttered the sublime prayer that follows.

* John xiv. 1-31.

continue in my love. If you keep my commandments, you will continue in my love; as I have kept my Father's commandments, and continue in his love. These things have I spoken to you, that my joy may be felt by you, and that your joy may be full. This is my commandment. That you love one another, as I have loved you. Greater love has no man than this, that he lays down his life for his friends. You are my friends, if you do what I command you. I call you no more servants, for the servant knows not what his master is doing; but I have called you friends, for all that I have heard of my Father I have made known to you. You have not chosen me, but I have chosen you, and ordained you to go and bring forth fruit, such fruit as may be lasting, so that whatever you may ask of the Father in my name, he may give you.

"This I command you, that you love one another. If the world hates you, you know that it hated me before it hated you. If you were of the world, the world would love its own; but, because you are not of the world, the world hates you. Remember what I said to you. The servant is not greater than his master. If they have persecuted me, they will persecute you also. If they have kept my words, they will keep yours also. But all this they will do to you for my sake, because they know not him who sent me. If I had not come and taught them, they would not be thus guilty; but now they have no excuse for their sin. He who hates me hates my Father also. If I had not done among them such works as no other man ever did, they would not be thus guilty; but now, though they have seen my works, they have hated both me and my Father. But thus is fulfilled what is written in their Law, "They hated me without a cause." But when the Comforter has come, whom I will send to you from the Father, the Spirit of Truth, which goes forth from the Father, he will testify of me. And you also will bear testimony, because you have been with me from the beginning.*

"These things have I spoken to you that you may not fall away. They will put you out of their synagogues; yea, the time is coming that whoever kills you will think that he is doing God service. Thus they will do because they have known neither the Father, nor me.

"But this I tell you, that when the time has come you may remember that I said it to you. I have not said it to you before, because I have been with you. But now I am going to him that sent me; and no one of you asks me where I am going. But because I have said these things sorrow has filled your hearts. But I tell you in truth, it is better for you that I go; for if I go not the Comforter will not come to you; but if I go, I will send him to you. And when he is come, he will convict the world of sin, of righteousness, and of judgment. Of sin, because they believe not on me. Of righteousness, because I am going to my Father, and you will see me no more. Of judgment, because the ruler of this world has been judged.

"I have yet much to say to you, but you cannot bear it now. However, when he, the Spirit of Truth, has come, he will guide you into all the truth; for he will not speak from himself, but will speak what he hears;

* John xv. 1-27.

and he will explain to you things that are coming. He will glorify me; for he will receive of mine, and give it to you. Whatever the Father has is mine; therefore I said, he will take what is mine, and give it to you. After a little while, and you will not see me; and again after a little while, you will see me, because I am going to the Father."

Then some of his disciples said to themselves, "What is the meaning of this that he says: 'A little while, and you will not see me, and again after a little while, you will see me; and I am going to the Father?'" They said, "What is this little while of which he speaks? We cannot tell."

Now Jesus knew that they were desirous to ask him, and he said to them, "Do you inquire among yourselves of that I said, 'After a little while, and you will not see me; and again after a little while, and you will see me? Truly, truly, I say to you, you will weep and lament, but the world will rejoice; and you will be sorrowful, but your sorrow will be turned into joy. A woman in travail has sorrow, because her hour has come; but when she is delivered, she forgets the anguish for joy that a man is born into the world. And so now you will sorrow, but I shall see you again, and your hearts will rejoice, and your joy no man will take from you. And then you will have no need to question me.

"Truly, truly, I say to you, whatever you shall ask the Father in my name, he will give you. Hitherto you have asked nothing in my name; ask and you shall receive, that your joy may be complete. I have spoken to you in dark sayings; but the time comes when I shall no more speak to you in dark sayings, but shall show you plainly concerning the Father. Then you will ask in my name; and I say not that I will pray the Father for you. For the Father himself loves you, because you have loved me, and have believed that I came forth from God. I came forth from the Father, and came into the world; now I am leaving the world, and going to my Father."

His disciples said to him, "Lo! now you speak plainly, and not in dark sayings. Now are we sure that you know all things, and need not that any man should question you; by this we believe that you came forth from God."

Jesus answered them, "Do you now believe? Lo! the hour is coming, yea, has now come, when you all will be scattered, every one his own way, and will leave me alone; and yet I am not alone, for the Father is with me. These things I have spoken to you, that through me you might have peace. In the world you will have tribulation; but be of good courage, I have overcome the world." *

When Jesus had thus spoken he raised his eyes to heaven, and said, "Father, the hour has come: glorify thy Son, that thy Son also may glorify thee through the power that thou hast given him over all men, to give to as many as thou hast given him eternal life. And this is life eternal, to know thee the only true God, and Jesus Christ whom thou hast sent. I have glorified thee on the earth; I have finished the work which thou gavest me to do. And now, O Father, glorify thou me with thine own self, with the

* John xvi. 1-33.

glory which I had with thee before the world was. I have made thee known to the men whom thou hast given me out of the world; thine they were, and thou gavest them to me; and they have kept thy words. Now they know that all things whatever thou hast given me are of thee. For I have given to them the truths which thou gavest to me; and they have received them, and know surely that I came forth from thee, and believe that thou didst send me. I pray for them; I pray not for the world, but for those whom thou hast given me; for they are thine. So all that are mine are thine, and thine are mine; and they are my glory. And now I remain no more in the world; but these will remain in the world, while I come to thee. Holy Father, keep through thine own name those whom thou hast given me, that they may be one, as we are. While I was with them in the world, I kept them as thine; those that thou gavest me I have kept, and none of them is lost, but the Son of perdition; that the Scripture might be fulfilled. And now I am coming to thee, and these things I speak in the world, that the joy which is my portion may be felt by them. I have given them thy word; and the world has hated them, because they are not of the world, as I am not of the world. I pray thee not to take them out of the world, but to keep them from the evil. They are not of the world, as I am not of the world. Consecrate them to thyself through thy truth; thy word is truth. As thou hast sent me to the world, so I also send them to the world. And for their sakes I devote myself, that they also may be devoted to thee through the truth. Nor do I pray for these only, but also for all who may believe in me through their word; that they all may be one, as thou, Father, art in me, and I in thee, so they also may be one in us; that the world may believe that thou hast sent me. And the glorious work which thou gavest me I have given to them; that they may be one, even as we are one; I in them and thou in me, that they may be made completely one; so that the world may know that thou hast sent me, and hast loved them, as thou hast loved me. Father, I also would that they, whom thou hast given me might be with me where I am, that they may behold my glory which thou hast given me; for thou didst love me before the foundation of the world. O righteous Father, though the world has not known thee, I have known thee, and these have known that thou hast sent me. And I have made thee known to them, and will make thee known, so that the love with which thou hast loved me, may be in them, and I in them." *

When Jesus had spoken these words, and they had sung a hymn, he went forth with his disciples over the Kidron, to the Mount of Olives, and entered a garden

Kidron.—A deep valley close to Jerusalem, and between it and the Mount of Olives.

Gethsemane.—The word means a "garden;" and this was probably an enclosure of fig, olive, and pomegranate trees at the foot of the Mount of Olives, and from a half to three-fourths of a mile from the walls of the city. From Luke xxii. 39, and John xviii. 2; it appears that Jesus often resorted there with his disciples. A garden is now shown, in which are eight gigantic olives, as the identical place in which the scene that follows occurred.

*John xvii. 1-26.

called Gethsemane. And when he had come to the place he said to his disciples: "Sit ye here, while I go and pray yonder."

Then, taking with him Peter and James and John, he began to be sorely distressed, and in great agony. And he said to them, "My soul is exceedingly sorrowful, even to death. Tarry ye here, and watch with me." And going forward about a stone's cast, he fell on his face, and prayed, saying: "O, my Father, if it be possible, — and all things are possible with thee, — let this cup pass from me; nevertheless, not my will, but thine be done." And there appeared an angel to him from heaven, strengthening him. And being in agony, he prayed more earnestly, and his sweat was, as it were, great drops of blood falling down to the ground.

When he rose up from prayer he came to the disciples, and found them sleeping for sorrow. And he said to Simon: "What! Could you not watch with me one hour? Watch and pray that you enter not into trial; the spirit indeed is willing, but the flesh is weak."

Great drops of blood. — Dr. Doddridge in a note on this passage, remarks that: "Aristotle and Diodorus Siculus, both mention bloody sweats as attending some extraordinary agony of mind; and I find Loti, in his life of Pope Sextus V, and Sir John Chardin, in his history of Persia, mention a like phenomenon, to which Dr. Jackson adds another from Thuanus." Voltaire, speaking of Charles IX of France, in his Universal History, says: "He died in his thirty-fifth year. His disorder was of a very remarkable kind; the blood oozed out of all his pores. This malady, of which there have been no other instances, was owing to either excessive fear, or violent agitation, or to a feverish and melancholy temperament."

Then going away a second time, he prayed again, saying: "O, my Father, if this cup may not pass from me, but I must drink it, thy will be done." And returning he found them again asleep; for their eyes were heavy, and they knew not what to say to him. Leaving them, he went away and prayed a third time, saying the same words. Then he returned to the disciples, and said to them: "Sleep on now and take your rest. Lo! the hour has come,—the Son of Man is delivered into the hands of sinners. Rise, let us go forward. He who betrays me is at hand." *

Now Judas, who betrayed him, knew the place, for Jesus often resorted there with his disciples; and having received a band of soldiers and officers from the chief priests and elders of the people, he came there while Jesus was yet speaking, with a great multitude, carrying lanterns, and torches, and weapons. And having agreed upon a sign with them that the one he should kiss was he whom they should take and lead away safely, he went before the rest, directly up to Jesus, saying: "Hail, Master!" and kissed him. Jesus said to him: "Judas, betray you the Son of Man with a kiss?" Then, knowing all that was to befall him, he went forward, and said to them: "Whom seek you?" They answered, "Jesus of Nazareth." Jesus said to them, "I am he," and as he said to them, "I am he," they went backward, and fell to the ground. Then Jesus asked them again, "Whom seek you?" And they said: "Jesus of Nazareth." Jesus answered: "I told you, I am he. If, then, you seek

* Matt. xxvi. 36-46. Mark xiv. 32-42. Luke xxii. 39-46. John xviii. 1.

me, let these go away." (To fulfil what he had said: "Of those whom thou hast given me, I have lost none.").

Then those who were about him, seeing what would follow, said to him: "Lord, shall we smite with the sword?" And Simon Peter, having a sword, drew it, and smote the servant of the high priest, cutting off his ear. The servant's name was Malchus. Jesus said to Peter, "Put up your sword into its sheath, for all who take the sword, will perish by the sword. Shall I not drink the cup which my Father has given me? Think you I could not now call on him, and he would send me more than twelve legions of angels? But how then would the Scriptures be fulfilled? For thus it must be."

The captain of the band, and the officers of the Jews then took Jesus, and bound him; but saying to them, "Suffer me thus far," he touched the servant's ear, and healed him. Then he said to the chief priests and officers of the temple, who had come to take him, "Have you come out as against a thief, with swords and clubs? I was daily with you, teaching in the temple, and you took me not. But, this is your hour, and the power of darkness." Then all the disciples forsook him and fled.

They led him away, first to Annas, who was the

Annas had been high-priest, having been appointed by Quirinus, imperial governor of Judea, A. D., 7. He was removed, after holding office seven years, for assuming the power to execute the death penalty; but was soon afterwards succeeded by his son, Eleazer. Five of his sons, and one son-in-law, — Caiaphas, — were successively high priests; but Annas appears to have exercised the real prerogatives of the office. He lived to a great age.

father-in-law of Caiaphas, the high priest that year. (It was Caiaphas who had given counsel to the Jews, that it was better that one man should die for the people). And a certain young man, having only a linen cloth wrapped about his body, followed, and the soldiers laid hold of him; but he, leaving the linen cloth in their hands, fled from them naked. Simon Peter also followed at a distance, and so did another disciple. That other disciple was acquainted with the high-priest, and went in with Jesus to the court of the high-priest's house; but Peter stood without, at the door. Then the other disciple, (who was known to the high-priest,) came out, and speaking to the girl who kept the door, brought in Peter.

The servants, and the officers who had taken Jesus, having kindled a fire of coals in the midst of the hall, (for it was cold,) seated themselves together by the fire; and Peter stood with them, warming himself. The maid of the high-priest, who kept the door, seeing Peter as he stood in the light, looked earnestly at him, and said: "Surely this man was with Jesus of Galilee." But he denied it before them all, saying, "Woman, I know him not." And he went out into the porch, and another maid saw him, and said to those that were there, "This is one of them," but he again affirmed with an oath, "I do not know the man." About an hour after, one of the servants — a

A certain young man is supposed by many to have been Mark, the author of the Gospel. The "other disciple" was, undoubtedly, John.

Fire of coals. — Jewish houses were without fire-places, and were warmed by braziers set in the centre of the courts or inner apartments.

kinsman to him whose ear Peter had cut off, — said to him, "Surely you are a Galilean, — your speech betrays you. Did I not see you in the garden with him?" Then Peter began to curse and to swear, saying, "I know not the man." And immediately, while he was speaking, the cock crew. Then the Lord turned, and looked upon him; and Peter remembered the words he had said, how before the cock crew, he would deny him thrice; and going out he wept bitterly.*

The high-priest then asked Jesus concerning his disciples, and his teaching; and Jesus answered, "I have spoken openly to the world; I have ever taught in synagogues, and in the temple, where all the Jews resort, and have said nothing in secret; why, then, do you question me? Ask those who have heard what I have taught. Lo! they know what I have said."

On his saying this, one of the officers who stood by struck Jesus with the palm of his hand, saying: "Do you answer the high-priest thus?" Jesus said to him, "If I have spoken evil, testify to what is evil; but if well, why do you smite me?"

Then Annas sent him bound to Caiaphas, the high-priest; and as soon as it was day, the elders of the people — the chief priests and teachers of the Law, — met, and brought Jesus before their council. And the whole Sanhedrim sought false testimony against him, so as to put him to death; but they found none; for though many bore false witness against him, their testimony was not sufficient. At last two came who

* Matt. xxvi. 57, 58, 69-75. Mark xiv. 53, 66-72. Luke xxii. John xviii. 13-18: 25-27.

testified: "We have heard him say, 'I will destroy this temple made with hands, and within three days, will build another made without hands." But their testimony, too, did not agree together. Then the high-priest, rising up in the midst, questioned Jesus, saying, "Do you make no reply? What is this that these men testify against you?" But he held his peace, answering nothing. The high-priest then questioned him again, saying: "I adjure thee by the living God to tell us if thou art the Christ, the Son of God?" Jesus said to him, "If I tell you, you will not believe; and if I also question you, you will not answer, nor let me go. Nevertheless, I say to you, I am; and hereafter you will see the Son of Man seated at the right hand of God, and coming in the clouds of heaven." Then they all said, "You are, then, the Son of God?" He said to them, "You speak truly. I am." The high-priest then rent his clothes, saying: "He has spoken blasphemy! What need is there for further testimony? for we have heard his blasphemy. What is your judgment?" They all answered: "He is worthy of death." Then the men who held Jesus mocked him, and smote him, and spat upon him; and the servants struck him with the palms of their hands, and, covering his face, buffeted him, saying: "Prophesy to us, thou Christ, who it is that smites thee." And they reviled him with many other blasphemies.*

Then the whole Sanhedrim rose, and when they had again bound Jesus, led him away to the hall of judgment, and delivered him to Pontius Pilate, the

Pontius Pilate was appointed procurator of Judea by Tibe-

* John xviii. 19-24. Luke xxii. 63-71. Matt. xxvi. 59-68. Mark xvi. 55-65.

governor; and it was early in the morning. They did not enter the judgment hall, lest they should be defiled, and prevented from eating the Passover; but Pilate came out to them, and asked: "What accusation do you bring against this man?" They answered, "If he were not a malefactor, we would not have brought him to you." Then Pilate said to them, "Take him yourselves, and judge him according to your law." The Jews answered, "We have no authority to put any man to death." (That the words of Jesus, showing what kind of death he was to die, might be fulfilled.) Then they began to accuse him, saying: "He is raising sedition among the people, forbidding them to pay tribute to Cesar, and saying that he himself, is Christ — a King."

Then Pilate, going into the judgment hall, called Jesus to him, and asked, "Are you the King of the Jews?" Jesus said to him, "Ask you this of yourself, or have others spoken to you of me?" Pilate answered: "Am I a Jew? Your own nation, and the chief priests have brought you before me. What have you done?" Jesus answered: "My kingdom is not of this world; if my kingdom were of this world, my servants would have fought to prevent my being delivered to the Jews; but now is my kingdom not from hence." Then Pilate said to him, "You are a King, then?" Jesus answered, "You say truly, I am

rius, A. D., 25-6. He was very unpopular with the Jews, and on several occasions practised upon them great cruelties. He was finally, about the year 36, accused by them to the Emperor, and sent by Viterlius, President of Syria, to Rome to answer their accusations. There, finding Tiberius dead, and wearied out by his misfortunes, he, soon afterwards, destroyed himself.

a king. To this end was I born, and for this I came into the world, — to bear testimony to the truth. Every lover of the truth, hears my voice." Pilate said to him, "What is truth?"

On saying this he went out again to the Jews, and said to them, "I find him guilty of no crime." Then the chief priests accused him of many things; but Jesus answered nothing. Pilate said to him, "Hear you not how much they testify against you?" But Jesus answered not a word, so that Pilate was greatly astonished. Then he again said to the chief priests and the multitude: "I do not find him guilty of any crime." But they were the more violent, saying: "He is stirring up sedition among the people by his teaching, from Galilee, and through all Judea, even to this city." Then Pilate, when he heard the word Galilee, asked if he were a Galilean; and being told that he was of Herod's jurisdiction, he sent him to Herod, who was at this time in Jerusalem.

Herod rejoiced greatly at seeing Jesus, for he had desired to see him for a long time, having heard of him, and being in hopes that he would do some miracle. He put many questions to him; but Jesus gave him no answer, though the chief priests and teachers of the Law were present, vehemently accusing him. Then Herod and his followers reviled him, and, in mockery, arrayed him in a gorgeous robe, and sent him back to Pilate. And Pilate and Herod became friends together that very day; for before they had been at enmity.*

*Matt. xxvii. 1, 2, 11-14. Mark xv. 1-5. Luke xxiii. 1-12. John xviii. 28-38.

Then Pilate, calling together the chief priests, the rulers, and the people, said to them: "You have brought this man to me as one stirring up sedition among the people, and lo! having examined him before you, I do not find him guilty of the crimes of which you accuse him. Nor does Herod; for he has sent him back to us, and lo! he has done nothing worthy of death. I will, therefore, scourge him, and let him go."

Now, at that festival it was customary for the governor to release to the people a prisoner, — whoever they would. And at that time there was a notorious prisoner, named Barabbas, who lay bound with others for making a riot in the city, and for committing murder in the riot. Then Pilate said to the multitude, "You have a custom that I release to you a prisoner at the Passover. Whom will you that I release, Barabbas, or Jesus, who is called Christ?" For he knew that the chief priests had brought Jesus before him through malice. But the chief priests and elders moved the multitude to ask him to release Barabbas, and destroy Jesus; and they cried out all at once, "Away with this man, and release to us Barabbas."

Pilate's wife, while he was seated on the judgment-seat, sent to him, saying: "Have nothing to do with that righteous man; for I have suffered much this day in a dream on his account." Pilate, therefore, willing to release Jesus, said again to the people, "Which of the two will you that I release to you?" And they cried out, "Not this man, but Barabbas." Now, Barabbas was a robber. Pilate then said to them: "What, then, shall I do with Jesus, whom you call the

King of the Jews?" And they cried out, "Crucify him! Crucify him!" But he said to them, "Why? What crime has he done? I find him guilty of nothing worthy of death. I will, therefore, scourge him, and let him go." But, with vehement out-cries, they demanded that he should be crucified. Their voices, and those of the chief priests prevailed, and Pilate, seeing that what he had said availed nothing, but that, on the contrary, the multitude were growing tumultuous, took water, and washed his hands before them, saying, "I am guiltless of the blood of this innocent man. Look you to it." And all the people answered: "His blood be on us, and on our children." Then he released Barabbas to them, and ordering Jesus to be scourged, delivered him to be crucified.*

The soldiers of the governor then carried Jesus into the Pretorium, and calling together the whole band, they scourged him. Then, stripping him, they clothed him in a purple robe, and platting a crown of thorns, placed it on his head, and put a reed in his right hand, and bowing their knees before him, mocked him, saying: "Hail, King of the Jews." And they spat upon him, and struck him with their hands, and taking the reed, beat him on the head, and kneeling down again, paid him homage.†

Then Pilate came out again, and said to the multitude: "Lo! I am bringing him out to you, to let you know that I find him guilty of no crime." Then Jesus came out, wearing the crown of thorns, and the purple robe; and Pilate said to them, "Behold the man!"

*Luke xxii. 13-25. Matt. xvii. 15-26. John xviii. 39-40. Mark xv. 6-15.

†Matt. xxvii. 26-30. Mark xv. 15-19. John xix. 1-3.

Then, when the chief priests and their officers saw him, they cried out again, "Crucify him! Crucify him!" Pilate said to them, "Do you take him and crucify him; for I find him guilty of no crime." The Jews answered, "We have a law; and by our law he ought to die, because he has claimed to be the Son of God."

When Pilate heard this he was the more afraid, and going into the Pretorium again, he said to Jesus, "Whence are you?" Jesus gave him no answer. Then Pilate said to him, "Speak you not to me? Do you not know that I have power to crucify you, and power to let you go." Jesus answered: "You would have no power over me, were it not given you from above. Therefore, those who have delivered me to you have so much the greater sin."

Upon this Pilate became earnest to release him; but the Jews cried out, "If you let this man go, you are not Cesar's friend. Whoever sets himself up for a king opposes Cesar."

When Pilate heard this, he brought Jesus out, and sat down on the judgment-seat in a place called the Pavement (in Hebrew, *Gabbatha*,) and it was the preparation of the Passover, and about the hour of noon. And he said to the Jews, "Behold your King." But they cried out, "Away with him! Away with him! Crucify him!" Pilate said to them, "Shall I crucify your King?" The chief priests answered: "We have no king but Cesar." Then Pilate yielded him up to them to be crucified.*

Then Judas, who had betrayed him, seeing that he

*John xix. 4-16.

was condemned, repented, and carried back the thirty pieces of silver to the chief priests and elders, saying: "I have sinned in betraying innocent blood." But they said to him: "What is that to us? Look you to that." He cast down the pieces of silver in the temple, and went away and hanged himself. But the chief priests took the silver pieces, saying: "It is not lawful to put them into the sacred treasury, because they are the price of blood." And after consulting together, they bought with them the Potter's Field, to bury strangers in. Hence that field has been called, "The field of Blood," to this day. Then was fulfilled what was said by Jeremiah, the prophet: "And they took the thirty pieces of silver, the price of him who was valued, whom the children of Israel did value; and they gave them to the Potter's Field, as the Lord had appointed for them." *

When *the soldiers* had mocked Jesus, they took off the purple robe, and putting on him his own clothes, led him away to be crucified. And he, bearing his cross, went forth to a place called Calvary, (in Hebrew, Golgotha,) which means the place of a skull. But, as they were going out of the city, they found one Simon, a Cyrenean, (the father of Alexander and Rufus,) coming from the country; and on him they laid the cross, and compelled him to bear it after Jesus.

And a great multitude of the people followed him, and of women, who lamented and bewailed him; but Jesus turning to them, said, "Daughters of Jerusalem! Weep not for me! but weep for yourselves, and your children! For the days are coming when it will be

* Matt. xxvii 3-10.

said, 'Blessed are the barren, the wombs that never bore, and the breasts that never gave suck.' Then they will say to the mountains, 'Fall on us,' and to the hills, 'Cover us.' For if they do this to the green tree, what will they do to the dry?"

Two others, who were malefactors, were led away with him to be put to death. And when they came to the place called Calvary, they gave him wine mingled with gall; but when he had tasted it, he would not drink. There they crucified him; and the male-

They crucified him. — "Crucifixion was inflicted by the Romans on servants, robbers, assassins, and rebels. The person subjected to this punishment was stripped of all clothing, except a band about the loins. In this state he was beaten, and was then obliged to carry his cross to the place of execution. The cross was an upright beam, with a horizontal cross-piece. A piece of wood projected from the upright beam, and on this the sufferer sat, since the weight of the body might, otherwise, have torn away the hands from the nails driven through them. The cross seldom exceeded ten feet in height. When it has been firmly fixed in the ground, the criminal was raised to the seat, and his hands were nailed to the cross-piece, and nailed through the palms. He usually remained suspended until he died, and the corpse became putrid; but in Judea, to comply with the law in Deut. xxi. 22, 23, the crucified were buried on the day of execution. When it was likely they would not die on that day, death was hastened by kindling a fire underneath the victim, by breaking his bones, or by piercing him with a spear. The Romans were accuustomed to give the criminal a medicated drink of wine and myrrh to produce intoxication, and lessen his pains. This was the drink which Jesus refused. The vinegar afterwards given him on a reed was, probably a mixture of sour wine and water, — the common beverage of the Roman soldiers."

factors, one on his right hand the other on his left; and thus the Scripture was fulfilled which says, "He was numbered with the transgressors."

Then Jesus said: "Father, forgive them; for they know not what they do."

When the soldiers had nailed him to the cross, they took his cloak, and divided it into four parts, one for each soldier, and also his tunic. Now his tunic was without seam, being woven in one piece from the top; so they said to one another: "Let us not rend it, but cast lots to see whose it shall be;" that the words of the prophet might be fulfilled: "They parted my raiment among them, and did cast lots for my vesture."

These things the soldiers did, and sitting down they watched him. Pilate also wrote an inscription, and had it put on the cross, over his head. And the inscription was, — in Greek, Latin and Hebrew, — "JESUS OF NAZARETH, THE KING OF THE JEWS."

This inscription was read by many of the Jews; for the place where Jesus was crucified was near the city. Then the chief priests said to Pilate, "Let not the inscription be, 'the King of the Jews,' but that he said, 'I am the King of the Jews." Pilate answered: "What I have written, I have written." *

And the passers-by reviled Jesus, nodding their heads, and saying: "Ah! thou that canst destroy the temple, and build it in three days, save thyself. If thou art the Son of God, come down from the cross." So also the chief priests, jesting with the Scribes and elders, said: "He saved others, cannot he save him-

* Matt. xxvii. 31-38. Mark xv. 29-28. Luke xxiii. 26, 34-38. John xix. 16-24.

self? If he is the King of Israel, let him now come down from the cross, and we will believe him. He trusted in God; let Him deliver him now if he desires him; for he said: 'I am the Son of God.'" The soldiers, too, mocked him, coming and offering him vinegar, saying, "If thou art the King of the Jews, save thyself." And one of the malefactors who were crucified with him reviled him, saying: "If you are the Christ, save yourself and us." But the other rebuked him, saying, "Do you not fear God, seeing you are in the same condemnation. And we indeed, justly, for we are receiving the due reward of our deeds; but this man has done nothing amiss." And he said to Jesus: "Remember me when you come into your kingdom." Jesus said to him, "Truly, I tell you, to-day you shall be with me in Paradise."

And by the cross of Jesus stood his mother, and his mother's sister, Mary the wife of Cleophas, and Mary of Magdala. Then Jesus, when he saw his mother, and the disciple whom he loved standing near, said to his mother, "Woman, behold! Thy Son!" Then he said to the disciple, "Behold! Thy mother." And from that hour the disciple took her to his own home.*

And it was about the sixth hour, and there was darkness over all the land till the ninth hour. And at the ninth hour Jesus cried with a loud voice, saying: "Eloi, Eloi, lama sabachthani?" that is to say: "My God? My God! Why hast thou forsaken me?" And some of those who stood near, when they heard it, said, "Lo! he calls for Elias." After this, Jesus,

*Matt. xxvii. 39-44. Mark xv. 29-32. Luke xxiii. 35-37; 39-43. John xix. 25-27.

knowing that all things had been accomplished, that the Scripture might be fulfilled, said: "I thirst!" And one of them ran, and filling a sponge with vinegar from a vessel standing near, put it on a stick of hyssop, and raised it to his mouth; but the others said, "Let alone; let us see if Elijah will come to save him."

Then, when Jesus had received the vinegar, he said, "It is finished," and crying out with a loud voice, "Father, into thy hands I commit my spirit," he bowed his head, and gave up the Ghost.*

And lo! the vail of the Sanctuary was torn asunder from the top to the bottom, and the earth quaked, and the rocks were rent, and the graves were opened, and many bodies of the saints who had fallen asleep, arose, and coming out of the tombs, after his resurrection, went into the holy city, and appeared to many. And when the centurion and those with him keeping watch over Jesus, saw the earth quake, and heard Jesus so cry out, they were struck with terror, and said: "Truly, this was the Son of God." And all the people who had flocked together to the sight, beholding what had happened returned, beating their breasts.

And standing at a distance, looking on, were all who had been connected with him, and the women who, when he was in Galilee, followed and ministered to him. Among them were Mary of Magdala, and Mary, the mother of James the less, and Joses, and Salome, and the mother of Zebedee's children, and

The vail of the Sanctuary. See Exodus xxvi. 31-33.

* Matt. xxvii. 45-50. Mark xv. 33-37. Luke xxiii. 44-46. John xix. 28-30.

many others, who had accompanied him to Jerusalem.*

Then the Jews, as it was the preparation day, that the bodies might not remain on the cross during the Sabbath, (for that Sabbath, was a great day,) besought Pilate that their legs might be broken, and they be taken away. Then the soldiers came and broke the legs of the first, and of the other who was crucified with Jesus. But when they came to Jesus, they saw that he was dead already, and broke not his legs. But one of the soldiers with a spear pierced his side, and at once there came out blood and water. These things were done that the Scripture might be fulfilled, "A bone of him shall not be broken." And again another Scripture which says, "They will look on him whom they have pierced."

And it being now evening, and the day of preparation, that is, the day before the Sabbath, Joseph of Arimathea, an honorable man, a member of the Sanhedrim, and a disciple of Jesus, (but secretly, for fear of the Jews,) who had not consented to the council or deed of the others, went, and going in boldly to Pilate, craved the body of Jesus. Pilate wondered if he were already dead, and sending for the centurion, inquired if he had been dead long. And being informed by the centurion, Pilate gave the body to Joseph. And Nicodemus, (who at the first came to Jesus by night,) brought a mixture of myrrh and aloes,—about a hun-

"*Blood and water.*—The thin membrane which surrounds the heart, called the *pericardium*, was the part pierced, and from this would flow lymph and blood."—JAHN.

* Matt. xxvii. 37-56. Mark xv. 38-41. Luke xxiii. 45, 47-49.

dred pounds, — and together, they took down the body of Jesus and swathed it in fine linen, with the aromatics, according to the Jews' mode of interment. And near the place where he was crucified, there was a garden, and in the garden there was, belonging to Joseph, a new tomb, hewn out of a rock, in which no one had ever been laid. There, then, it being the preparation day, they laid Jesus, because the tomb was near at hand; and rolling a great stone against the door of the tomb, they departed.

And the women who came from Galilee — Mary of Magdala, and Mary the mother of Joses, — followed, and sitting over against the tomb, saw how the body was laid.*

On the next day, (that following the day of the preparation,) the chief priests and the Pharisees went in a body to Pilate, saying: "Sir, we remember that this deceiver while living, said, 'In three days I shall rise again.' Give command, therefore, that the sepulchre be made secure until the third day, lest his disciples should come by night, and steal him away, and say to the people, 'He has been raised from the dead,' so the last error should be worse than the first." Pilate said to them, "You have a guard; go and make it as sure as you can." So they went and made the sepulchre secure, sealing the stone, and setting a watch.†

* Matt. xxvii. 57-61. Mark xv. 42-47. Luke xxiii. 50-56. John xix. 31-42.

† Matt. xxvii. 62-66.

PART NINTH.

FROM THE RESURRECTION TO THE ASCENSION.

LIFE OF JESUS.

PART NINTH.

AND Mary of Magdala, and the other Mary, returning to the city, prepared spices and ointments, and rested on the Sabbath, according to the commandment. Then, while it was yet dark, on the morning of the first day of the week they went with certain others to the tomb, carrying the perfumes they had prepared. And they said to one another, "Who will roll away the stone for us from the door of the tomb?" for it was very large. But, on looking, they saw that the stone had been rolled away; and entering the tomb they found not the body of the Lord Jesus. For lo! there had been a great earthquake, and an angel of the Lord, descending from heaven, had rolled back the stone from the door, and sat upon it. His countenance was like lightning, and his raiment white as snow, and at the sight of him the guard were struck with terror, and became as dead men.*

Then Mary of Magdala, seeing the stone rolled away from the tomb, ran to Simon Peter, and to the other disciple whom Jesus loved, and said to them "They have taken the Lord out of the tomb, and

* Mark xvi. 1. Matt. xxviii. 2-4.

we know not where they have laid him." But while *the other women* were in great perplexity, concerning this, lo! two men stood by them in glittering garments, and they were terrified, and bowed their faces to the earth; but the men said to them, "Fear not; ye seek Jesus of Nazareth who was crucified. He is not here; but has risen. Remember what he said to you while he was yet in Galilee; that the Son of Man would be betrayed into the hands of sinful men, and be crucified, and the third day would rise again. Come, see the place where the Lord lay; and go quickly, and tell his disciples and Peter, that he has risen from the dead, and goes before you into Galilee. There shall you see him. Lo! we have told you."

And the women remembered the words of the Lord, and departing quickly from the tomb, with fear and great joy, ran to give his disciples word.*

Meanwhile Peter set out with the other disciple, to go to the tomb, and both ran together, but the disciple outran Peter, and coming first to the tomb, stooped down and saw the grave-clothes lying there, but did not go in. Then came Simon Peter following him, and entered the tomb and saw the grave-clothes lying, and the napkin that was about his head, not lying with the grave-clothes, but wrapped up in a place by itself. Then the other disciple who came first to the tomb, went in also, and saw and believed. For as yet they understood not the Scripture, that he must rise from the dead.†

Then the disciples returned to their homes wonder-

*Matt. xxviii. 1, 5-7. Mark xvi. 1, 2-7. Luke xxiv. 1-8. John xx. 1, 2.

†John xx. 3-10. Luke xxiv. 12.

ing at what had taken place; but Mary remained standing without by the tomb, weeping. As she was weeping, she stooped down to look into the tomb, and saw two angels, arrayed in white, sitting, the one at the head, and the other at the foot, where the body of Jesus had lain. And they said to her, "Woman, why weep you?" She said to them: "Because they have taken away my Lord, and I know not where they have laid him." Saying this she turned back, and saw Jesus standing by but knew not that it was Jesus. Jesus said to her: "Woman, why weep you? Whom are you seeking?" She, supposing him to be the gardener, said to him, "Sir, if you have carried him hence, tell me where you have laid him, and I will take him away." Jesus said to her, "Mary." She turned and said to him: "Rabboni," — which means Teacher. Jesus said to her, "Touch me not; for I have not yet ascended to my Father; but go to my brothers, and tell them that I am about to ascend to my Father and your Father, to my God and your God."

Then Mary of Magdala went and told the disciples that she had seen the Lord, and he had said these things to her; but when they heard that he was alive, and she had seen him, they believed not.*

And as the *other women* went to tell the disciples, Lo! Jesus met them and said, "All hail." And they went near, and laid hold of his feet, falling on the ground before him. Then Jesus said to them, "Be not afraid; go and tell my brothers to depart into Galilee, and there they shall see me." And they returned

*John xv. 11-18. Mark xvi. 9-11.

and told all to the eleven, and to the rest; but their words seemed to them as idle tales, and they believed them not.*

As the women were going, some of the guard entered the city, and told the chief priests all that had taken place. And they, having assembled with the elders, and consulted together, gave a large sum of money to the soldiers, saying, "Tell the people his disciples came by night, and stole him away while you were asleep; and, should the governor hear of this, we will satisfy him, and keep you from trouble." So they took the money, and did as they were told; and that story has been current among the Jews to this day.†

Then he was seen of Cephas; and after that, the same day, he appeared in another form, to two of them as they went into the country, to a village called Emmaus, distant from Jerusalem about threescore furlongs. And as they talked together of all that had happened, Jesus himself drew near, and went with them; but their eyes were held so that they did not know him. And he said to them, "What is this that you discourse about with one another, as you walk and are sad?" One of them, whose name was Cleopas, answered him, "Are you such a stranger in Jerusalem as not to know the things which have happened in these few days?" He said to them, "What things?" They said to him, "Those concerning Jesus of Nazareth, who was a prophet mighty in deed and word before God, and all the people; how our chief priests and rulers caused him to be con-

*Matt. xxviii. 8-10. Mark xiv. 8. Luke xxiv. 9-11.
†Matt. xxviii. 11-15.

demned to death, and crucified him. But we trusted that it was he who was to have redeemed Israel; and besides all this, to-day is the third day since these things took place. But certain women of our company have astonished us; for going early in the morning to the tomb they found not his body, but came saying they had seen a vision of angels, who said that he was living. And one of those with us, who went to the tomb, found it even as the women had said; but him they saw not."

Then Jesus said to them, "How slow of heart ye are to believe all that the prophets have spoken! Was it not necessary for Christ through these sufferings to enter into his glory?" And beginning with Moses, and all the prophets, he expounded to them in all the Scriptures the things concerning himself.

And when they came near to the village to which they were going, he made as though he would go further. But they pressed him, saying: "Remain with us, for it is toward evening, — the day is far spent." And he went in to tarry with them.

And while he was at table with them, he took the bread, and blessed it, and broke it and gave it to them. Then their eyes were opened, and they knew him; and he vanished out of their sight.

And they said to one another, "Did not our hearts burn within us while he talked with us on the road, and explained to us the Scriptures?" And immediately they returned to Jerusalem, and found the eleven, and those that were with them, assembled together at table, who told them that the Lord had indeed risen, and appeared to Simon. And they told what happened on the road, and how he had become known to them while breaking bread.*

While they were thus talking, the doors where they were assembled being shut for fear of the Jews, Jesus came and stood in their midst, and said to them, "Peace be with you." But they were startled and terrified, and thought that they saw a spirit. And he said to them, "Why are you troubled? and why do doubts arise in your minds? Behold my hands and my feet, that it is I, myself; touch me and see, for a spirit has not flesh and bones as you see me have." Saying this, he showed them his hands, his feet, and his side. While they were still in doubt through joy and wonder, he said to them: "Have you anything to eat?" And they gave him a piece of broiled fish and of a honey comb, and taking it, he ate before them. Then the disciples rejoiced when they saw the Lord.

And he said to them: "This is what I told you while I was yet with you, that it was necessary that all that is written in the Law of Moses, in the Prophets, and in the Psalms concerning me, should be accomplished." Then he opened their minds to understand the Scriptures, and said to them, "Thus it is written, and thus it was necessary that Christ should suffer, and rise from the dead on the third day; and that repentance and remission of sins should be preached in his name to all nations, beginning at Jerusalem. And you are the witnesses of these things."

Then he said to them again, "Peace be with you. As my Father has sent me, so send I you. Go ye into

* 1 Cor. xv. 5. Luke xxiv. 16-35. Mark xvi. 12, 13.

all the world, and proclaim the glad tidings to every creature. He who believes and is baptized, will be saved; he who believes not will be condemned. And these signs shall accompany those who believe; in my name they will cast out demons; they will speak with new tongues; they will take up serpents; if they drink any deadly thing it will not hurt them, and they will lay hands on the sick, and they will recover."

And after saying this, he breathed on them, and said, "Receive ye the Holy Spirit. Whosesoever sins you may remit, are remitted, and whosesoever sins you may retain, are retained." *

But Thomas, called Didymus, one of the twelve, was not with them when Jesus came. Then the other disciples said to him, "We have seen the Lord." But he said to them, "Unless I see in his hands the print of the nails, and put my finger into the print of the nails, and put my hand to his side, I shall not believe." And eight days after, his disciples being again in the house, and Thomas with them, Jesus came, the doors being closed, and standing in the midst of them, said, "Peace be with you." Then he said to Thomas, "Reach hither your finger, and see my hands; and reach hither your hand, and put it to my side; and be not faithless, but believing." Thomas answered him, "My Lord and my God." Jesus said to him, "Thomas, because you have seen me, you have believed; blessed are they who, without seeing me, have believed."†

* Mark xvi. 14-18. 1 Cor. xv. 5. Luke xxiv. 36-49. John xx. 19-23.

† John xx. 24-29.

After this the eleven disciples went away to Galilee, and Jesus showed himself again to them, by the lake of Tiberias; and in this manner he showed himself. There were together Simon Peter, and Thomas, called Didymus, and Nathaniel of Cana, in Galilee, and the two sons of Zebedee, and two others of his disciples. Simon Peter said to them: "I am going a fishing." They said to him: "We too will go with you." They went and entered a boat; but that night they caught nothing. And when it was morning, Jesus stood on the shore; but the disciples knew not that it was Jesus. Then Jesus said to them, "Children, have you any fish?" They answered him, "No." He said to them, "Cast the net on the right side of the boat, and you will find them." Then they cast it, and were not able to draw it because of the great number of fishes. Then that disciple whom Jesus loved said to Peter, "It is the Lord!" When Simon Peter heard that it was the Lord, he girt round him his fisher's coat, (for he was without his cloak,) and cast himself into the lake. But the other disciples came in the boat — for they were only about two hundred cubits from the shore, — dragging the net with the fishes. As soon as they were at the land, they saw a fire of coals, and a fish lying upon it, and a loaf of bread. Jesus said to them, "Bring some of the fish which you have just caught." Simon Peter went on board the boat, and drew the net to land, full of great fishes, a hundred and fifty and three; and though there were so many, the net was not broken. Jesus said to them, "Come and breakfast?" And none of the disciples durst ask him who he was, knowing that it was the Lord. Then

Jesus came and took the bread, and distributed it to them, and the fish also.

This was the third time that Jesus showed himself to his disciples, after he had risen from the dead.

When they had breakfasted, Jesus said to Simon Peter, "Simon, son of Jonah, do you love me more than these love me?" He answered, "In truth Lord, you know that I love you." Jesus said to him: "Feed my lambs." Again he said to him a second time: "Simon, son of Jonah, do you love me?" He answered him, "In truth, Lord, you know that I love you." Jesus said to him, "Feed my sheep." He said to him a third time, "Simon, son of Jonah, do you love me?" Peter was grieved because he asked him a third time, "Do you love me;" and he answered, "Lord, you know all things; you know that I love you." Jesus said to him, "Feed my sheep. Truly, truly, I tell you, when you were young, you girt yourself and walked where you would; but when you shall be old, you will stretch forth your hands, and others will gird you, and carry you when you would not." This he spoke, signifying by what death Peter would glorify God. And when he had spoken thus, he said to him, "Follow me." Then Peter, turning about, saw the disciple whom Jesus loved following; (the one who at the supper leaned on the breast of Jesus, and said, 'Lord, who is it that betrays thee?') Peter seeing him, said to Jesus, "Lord, and what shall this man do?" Jesus said to him, "If I will that he remain till I come, what is that to you? Follow me."

From this the report went abroad among the brothers, that this disciple was not to die; but Jesus said not, "He shall not die; but, if I will that he remain till I come, what is that to you?" *

After this he was seen on a mountain where Jesus had appointed, by more than five hundred brethren at once, of whom the greater remain to this time, but some have fallen asleep. And when they saw him they prostrated themselves before him; but some were in doubt. Then Jesus, coming near them, said: "All power is given to me in heaven and on earth. Go ye, therefore, and teach all nations, baptizing them in the name of the Father, and of the Son, and of the Holy Spirit; teaching them to observe all things that I have commanded you; and Lo! I am with you always, to the end of the world."†

After this he was seen of James, then of all the apostles, to whom he showed himself alive by many infallible proofs, being seen by them forty days, and speaking of the things pertaining to the kingdom of God. And being assembled with them he directed them not to depart from Jerusalem, but to wait for the promise of the Father, which he said, "Ye have heard of me. For John truly baptized with water; but you shall be baptized with the Holy Ghost not many days hence." When they were then together, they asked him, "Lord, wilt thou at this time restore the kingdom to Israel?" He said to them, "It is not for you to know the times or the seasons which the Father has in his own power. But you shall receive power after the Holy Ghost has come upon you; and you shall be

* Matt. xxviii. 16. John xxi. 1-24.

† Matt. xxviii. 16-20. 1 Cor. xv. 6.

my witnesses in Jerusalem, and in all Judea, and in Samaria, and to the utmost ends of the earth." *

And leading them out as far as Bethany, he lifted up his hands and blessed them. And while he blessed them he was taken up, and a cloud received him out of their sight; and being carried up into heaven, he sat down on the right hand of God.

And as they looked intently towards heaven, while he was going up, Lo! two men stood by them in white apparel, who said: "Ye men of Galilee, why stand ye gazing up into heaven? This Jesus who is taken up from you into heaven shall so come, in like manner as ye have seen him go into heaven."

Then they returned with great joy to Jerusalem, from the Mount called Olivet, — which is distant from Jerusalem a Sabbath-day's journey, — and were continually in the temple praising and blessing God. And they went forth, and preached everywhere, the Lord working with them, and confirming their teaching by accompanying miracles.†

* 1 Cor. xv. 7. Acts i. 3-8.

† Luke xxiv. 50-53. Mark xvi. 19, 20. Acts i. 9-12.

www.ingramcontent.com/pod-product-compliance
Lightning Source LLC
LaVergne TN
LVHW010227110826
845151LV00004B/1216
* 9 7 8 1 4 2 5 5 2 6 7 2 6 *